How To Study The Bible

New Directions for Studying the Word of God

Charles W. Ford

RadiantBOOKS

Gospel Publishing House/Springfield, Mo. 65802

02-0912

© 1978 by the Gospel Publishing House
Springfield, Missouri 65802.
Adapted from *How to Study the Bible* by G. Raymond Carlson
© 1964 by the Gospel Publishing House. All rights reserved.
Library of CongressCatalog Card Number 77-99213
ISBN 0-88243-912-X
Printed in the United States of America.

A teacher's guide for individual or group study with this book is
available from the Gospel Publishing House (order number 32-0183).

Contents

1
What's in It for Me?

Since he was new in the community, the high school principal wanted to project a positive image. He and his family had moved into the area 2 months prior to the opening of school. The parent-teacher association had planned an afternoon social to welcome them to the community. Their 11-year-old son was ill and not able to attend the affair. During the afternoon the president of a very prominent local service club called to invite the principal to join their organization. The boy answered the telephone. After listening to various ways his father could serve people in the town and to the later embarrassment of his father, he very bluntly asked: "But what's in it for us?"

What should I get out of reading or studying the Bible? This is a valid question that many today are asking. Those who ponder this question deserve a clear answer. In our modern society, time is at a premium. Mothers are busy with household chores, young people find the challenges of school time-consuming, while fathers work overtime to provide for their families. Career people too find time a precious commodity. Consequently, only items of high priority command our attention. So—what's in Bible study for me? Why should I make room for it in my busy life?

An Exciting Experience

Bible study should be an exciting and adventurous experience. The Word of God contains stories of every description. Romance, war, adventure, poverty, wealth, tragedy, and happiness are only a few of the topics covered in this marvelous Book. These subjects are woven into a beautiful pattern of spiritual truth by the writers. A careful analysis of this pattern reveals the most interesting and exciting events in the history of man. The heart of a Christian should be filled with anticipation as he searches the Scriptures. Truths more precious than emeralds or diamonds await the serious student.

Don't be discouraged if you haven't had the privilege of higher education. The study of Greek, Hebrew, and systematic theology is interesting and helpful, but not indispensable. The Bible was planned, inspired, and brought into being by God. It is designed for all people—the rich, the poor, the educated, and the uneducated. Its most precious truths can be found by any student motivated by an attitude of eagerness and sincerity.

Eternal Life

"Search the Scriptures; for in them ye think ye have eternal life: and they are they which testify of me" (John 5:39). Modern man in his quest for ultimate reality has often looked to sources other than the Bible. His search has led him into philosophy, science, education, theology, and even the occult. None of these has filled the longing in his heart or quenched his desire for spiritual reality.

Why is it that eternal life can be found and experienced by studying the Scriptures? What is so unique about them? Jesus himself answered these questions. According to His own words the Scriptures testify of Him or point to Him. The writer to the Hebrews also comments on this: "And being made perfect, he became the author of eternal salvation unto all them that obey him" (5:9).

So, the greatest experience a human being can have awaits the earnest student of the Word of God. Learning about Jesus' birth, early life, and powerful ministry should arouse feelings of admiration and appreciation in any sincere reader. As we follow Jesus' earthly life as portrayed in the Gospels, and as we watch Him compassionately reaching out to the poor, the sick, and the spiritually blind, we are motivated to continue our search of the Scriptures.

Yes, you can learn about Jesus in the Scriptures. But even more important, you can receive eternal life through learning to know Him personally.

Which Way, Please?

One major problem common to all Christians is determining God's plan for their lives. Regardless of your age, God has a vital interest in the decisions you make momentarily and the long-range plans you have for your life. We must always remember that God did not save us and then leave the details of our lives to chance. There is a definite place in His kingdom for you. No Christian, at any stage in life, is set on the shelf or retired by our Heavenly Father. There is a niche for every believer in God's great program on earth. To find God's plan and to follow it is the highest course any individual Christian can pursue.

A pastor made a similar statement while teaching a class of young adults during the Sunday school hour. He was pleasantly surprised to discover that his students almost unanimously agreed with him. However, while they agreed on the statement, they expressed deep concern about how to find God's plan for their individual lives. Needless to say, the remainder of the class session was given to a profitable discussion about finding God's will. Maybe this problem has troubled you just as it has many other earnest Christians. And you too at times have prayed: "Which way do you want me to go, Lord?"

There is no better way to find God's plan for your life than to study the Bible and pray. The Bible is filled with the knowledge of what God wants for His followers. The Psalmist expresses this clearly: "Thy word is a lamp unto my feet, and a light unto my path" (Psalm 119:105). A believer who consistently studies the Bible will seldom be perplexed about knowing what God would have him do.

What Kind of Reflection?

Most people make efficient use of a piece of grooming equipment called a mirror each morning before going out into the world of activity. This marvelous device provides us with a glimpse of ourselves as we prepare to enter the social world. We are not always pleased with our first look in the morning. Even after the grooming process is under way and adjustments in our appearance have been made, we are not completely satisfied.

As one can view his physical appearance in a mirror, so he can see his spiritual reflection in the Bible. The apostle Paul in admonishing Timothy wrote: "All Scripture is given by inspiration of God, and is profitable for doctrine, for reproof, for correction, for instruction in righteousness: that the man of God

may be perfect, thoroughly furnished unto all g'
works" (2 Timothy 3:16, 17).

The earnest student will see reflections of his spiritual life in the Word of God. What a beautiful way God has of revealing areas of our lives where adjustments should be made. When we sincerely sing choruses such as "Oh! To Be Like Thee," we can expect God to give us glimpses of ourselves in the mirror of His Word. The encouraging fact is that we not only see our shortcomings and weaknesses but also the remedy for them.

You should not be too discouraged when glaring imperfections are revealed by the divine mirror. It is because God cares about you. He is concerned about every phase of your life. The reflections we see are God's way of revealing areas where adjustments are necessary to improve the spiritual quality of our life. Before succumbing to discouragement, remember the Scripture passage: "Being confident of this very thing, that he which hath begun a good work in you will perform it until the day of Jesus Christ" (Philippians 1:6).

Questions, Questions, Questions

Where did the earth come from? How did plants, animals, and man get started on earth? Who am I and what is the purpose of my life? These are questions that have plagued the human mind for centuries. Philosophers, theologians, and scientists theorize about them while common people grope for answers. Many classroom discussions focus on these questions as students and teachers alike seek solutions. Volumes have been written by supposed authorities in an attempt to satisfy the human mind.

Charles Darwin, the celebrated naturalist of the

ury, offered his *Origin of the Species* as an
to some of these questions. Many scientists
d Darwin's evolutionary view of Creation.
modified his teachings and offered them to
the world as solutions. Modern theologians, in their
attempt to bridge the gap between the Genesis account of Creation and evolution, proposed a com-
promise called theistic evolution. According to
them, God used evolution as His method of Creation.

The maze of theories that followed only added to
man's confusion and perplexity. After years of
searching he is no closer to discovering answers than
when he started.

Much good to mankind has resulted from scientific
investigation, but there are some critical problems it
can never solve. Many of these problems are dealt
with in the Bible. Great questions relating to the
origin of animals and inanimate objects, along with
the purposes of human life, are not mysteries to the
student of God's Word. Although we may never
know all the details, the Bible offers answers that
satisfy the sincere inquiring mind.

The simple and clear declarations of Scripture relating to the universe, man, his origin, his purpose,
and his destiny are worthy of consideration by all
men. "In the beginning God created the heaven and
the earth" (Genesis 1:1). In this one profound but
easily understood sentence God declares how the
world came into existence. Although He does not
relate all the details of His creative work, the inspired account leaves no doubt as to who exercised
creative power.

Another classic and oft-quoted verse gives us a
deeper insight into the purposes of human existence: "For God so loved the world, that he gave his

only begotten Son, that whosoever believeth in him should not perish, but have everlasting life" (John 3:16).

So, as a student of the inspired Scriptures you have access to knowledge not available in any other volume. It may be necessary for you to dig and search and pray. If so, the results will indeed be rewarding. You will discover answers to questions that men throughout history have diligently sought. As you share this information with others, they too may learn to search the Scriptures as the primary source of knowledge.

God, Who Is He?

Historically, one of the greatest problems challenging the mind of man pivots on the question: Who is God? Closely related to it are questions such as: What is He like? Does He really care about man or does He seek to destroy him?

Universally, man in every generation has developed a theory about Deity and a system of religion. These theories and religions vary considerably but they have one thing in common: they represent man's longing and a need to know God. This expression of the heart can be seen in the works of ancient and modern man. When we read history, we cannot doubt their sincerity. But philosophies about God that originate in the minds of men do not satisfy the longings of the heart. Then, how can man learn about God?

Again, we go to the source of true knowledge, the Bible. God in this marvelous, inspired Book reveals himself to man. "God is a Spirit: and they that worship him must worship him in spirit and in truth" (John 4:24). This verse is only one of many through-

11

out the Bible that give us a glimpse of God and His characteristics or attributes. Let's look at just a few of these passages in which God reveals some aspect of himself.

One attribute of God is love: "And we have known and believed the love that God hath to us. God is love; and he that dwelleth in love dwelleth in God, and God in him" (1 John 4:16). This truth is sprinkled liberally throughout the Scriptures. Any earnest student will discern and comprehend this eternal truth as he reads the Bible.

"The eternal God is thy refuge" (Deuteronomy 33:27). Although the concept presents an unusual challenge to the human mind, the Scriptures declare that God is eternal. In simple terms it means He didn't have a beginning and His existence will never end. He has the quality of timelessness. If you can't entirely comprehend the meaning of eternity, don't despair. Many other earnest Bible scholars have pondered its meaning. Because the Bible has proven to be trustworthy, accept what it declares without question. It is not a book on sociology or science whose concepts are subject to change as research brings to light new facts and information.

Don't be disturbed when additional questions arise and you can't find the answer. First, God has not revealed everything about himself. Some things about God the Christian may never know during his earthly pilgrimage (Deuteronomy 29:29).

There probably is no area of knowledge where man has exhausted the facts. He has accomplished unbelievable and marvelous feats by using his mind and skills. But man does have limitations. God, in His wisdom, has revealed to man only the divine characteristics that are necessary for his understanding. Perhaps eternity will afford us greater oppor-

12

tunities to learn more about His beauty and majesty.

"Humble yourselves therefore under the mighty hand of God, that he may exalt you in due time: casting all your care upon him; for he careth for you" (1 Peter 5:6, 7). Through the ages unregenerate man could not decide whether or not his god really cared for him. At times his god was conceived of as benevolent, but all too often he was seen as violent and fearsome.

The eternal God who revealed himself to man through the inspired Scriptures expresses His tender concern for human beings. What a beautiful declaration coming from the heart of God to man through one of His servants: "Casting all your care upon him; for he careth for you" (v. 7).

"And if it seem evil unto you to serve the LORD, choose you this day whom ye will serve" (Joshua 24:15). Contrary to many human concepts of God, He has given man the awesome power of choice. We get a glimpse of His tenderness and love as He invites man to serve Him, but doesn't use coercion.

Are you disturbed and perplexed by unanswered questions about God, the world, and yourself? Perhaps you have been seeking answers from the wrong source. Try the Bible. As millions have found, you will not be disappointed by your search; but rather, you will be delighted and blessed as the Holy Spirit illuminates your mind. You will discover answers to questions that will satisfy your mind and also your heart.

So, what's in Bible study for you? Knowledge, blessing, guidance, spiritual strength, and answers to the critical questions of life are only some of the benefits you will reap. The sincere student of the Bible is continually learning and growing in the grace of God.

2

Approach From the Right

Several years ago a pastor and his family were traveling through the western states. They had been on an extended vacation and were headed home. Their journey led them through an area that had been hit by a devastating storm. Power lines were down and some bridges and roads were washed out.

Late in the afternoon they rounded a curve and were confronted by a hurriedly made road sign that read: "CAUTION: Approach Only From the Right Lane." As they rounded the curve, there, easily visible to all, was a gigantic hole in the road that had been washed out by the heavy rains and flooding. Only the right lane was passable.

As you approach the Bible to read and study, one vital key to success is your attitude. An attitude is a state of mind or feeling about something. What you think and feel about the Bible will to a large degree determine the benefits you receive from studying it. So, approach this wondrous Book with the *right* attitude. What is the proper attitude a Christian should develop and maintain to make Bible study a spiritually profitable and enjoyable experience?

With Confidence

The information found in most books needs to be

carefully evaluated and sifted. This is particularly true of books written by secular authors, but it is also the case with some books written by religious authors. Even though a writer may be an authority in one area of knowledge, the reader cannot assume that all information contained in the book is true. Sometimes even well-meaning Christian authors have published articles and books that contain facts that are not completely Biblical or correct. Consequently, you must learn to evaluate a book's content in the light of what the Bible teaches. Then you will never go wrong.

Although most books need to be read guardedly, this does not apply to the Bible, the Word of God. It is unique among books. Every fact and every concept is true. You can read and study the Bible with complete confidence, knowing that the authors were moved and guided by the Holy Spirit. "For no prophecy recorded in Scripture was ever thought up by the prophet himself. It was the Holy Spirit within these godly men who gave them true messages from God" (2 Peter 1:20, 21, *The Living Bible*).

Will the Bible student sometimes encounter things he does not understand? Yes. Even many well-known evangelical scholars have experienced problems during the investigative process. God didn't intend for the answers to all great questions to come easily.

This is understandable when we view the broad scope and profound nature of the knowledge contained in the Bible. History, law, poetry, and biographies are only some of the areas dealt with, and they are woven into a beautiful pattern revealing the plan of redemption. These Books, although written over a period of about 1,600 years, contain information covering several thousands of years as well as prophetic glimpses into the future.

And so, even though you may not completely understand the meaning of a verse or passage, you can read with confidence. This is especially true when you realize your knowledge is increasing and your understanding is broadening each time you read the Word of God. Peter expressed this concept when he wrote: "But grow in grace, and in the knowledge of our Lord and Saviour Jesus Christ. To him be glory both now and for ever" (2 Peter 3:18). Each new nugget of truth often leads to a broader and deeper understanding of some other spiritual concept. Thus, we grow.

It is important to the Bible student to distinguish between not understanding a situation and doubting. Perhaps no individual Christian scholar has ever exhausted the field of Bible knowledge. But we should all be growing in knowledge and spiritual understanding. What a glorious adventure every believer can have searching the Bible for diamonds of spiritual truth! You can read and study and explore with complete confidence, knowing that every fact is true and will fit into a beautiful pattern. This pattern is a broadening understanding of God's plan and purpose for you and all mankind.

Anticipation

Unfortunately, many Christians read the Bible mainly out of a sense of duty. They have not yet discovered the excitement and great joy that fellowship in the Word can bring. Centuries before the Scriptures were completed and put into printed form, the Psalmist caught a glimpse of this truth. He wrote: "Thy word is very pure: therefore thy servant loveth it" (Psalm 119:140).

Meditating in God's Word was no burdensome chore to the writer of this verse. God's promises and Word had been thoroughly tested, tried, and proven. It was a delightful experience for the Psalmist to receive God's Word: "I rejoice at thy word, as one that findeth great spoil" (v. 162).

Christians today should have even more reason to find Bible study a delightful and spiritually enriching experience. First, we have available the complete revelation of God. The 66 Books that comprise our Bible have been printed in most languages of the world. The many versions, along with commentaries and other helps, make Bible study a spiritually rich endeavor.

Approach it with anticipation. Each encounter will reinforce old truths and often lead to the discovery of new ones. As you develop and foster this kind of approach and attitude, the burdensome duty of Bible reading will disappear. In its place will come a feeling of expectation and joy. It will then be easy to open the Word of God for a session of meditation, but difficult to close it.

Prayerfully

A young man of unusual brilliance attended a well-known Bible college several years ago. He graduated from high school near the top of his class and had won several awards for academic achievement. Because of his heavy schedule of classes, his prayer life suffered. As the school year progressed, he became increasingly argumentative and opinionated. Scholarship without the development of a prayer life often results in this kind of attitude.

17

Prayer was intended by the Master to go hand in hand with Bible study. It is an indispensable component of every Christian's spiritual life. Without it even Bible reading loses its true value.

The apostles, ministering to the Early Church as recorded in the Book of Acts, demonstrated this truth: "But we will give ourselves continually to prayer, and to the ministry of the word" (Acts 6:4). Their priorities are clearly stated in this verse. Continual prayer and ministry of the Word is a powerful combination.

Tremendous spiritual victories were won by the apostolic Christians because they exalted the Word of God and continued in prayer. The Holy Spirit, referring to the seven men chosen to administer the church's business, and speaking through Luke, declares: "Whom they set before the apostles: and when they had prayed, they laid their hands on them. And the word of God increased; and the number of the disciples multiplied in Jerusalem greatly" (vv. 6, 7).

Believers today who approach Bible study with a prayerful attitude can also expect spiritual victories.

Expectancy

A positive attitude contributes to success in most areas of life. Many people, including Christians, find it difficult to believe good will come from some situations they encounter in life. Gloom breeds gloom. Failure often breeds failure, unless there is a change of attitude. Consider what Jesus taught: "I tell you, then, whatever you ask for in prayer, believe that you have received it and it will be yours" (Mark 11:24, *New English Bible*).

Being positive is more than a mental attitude as

proposed by some psychologists. It was taught by the Lord Jesus Christ to His disciples almost 2,000 years ago. He encouraged the disciples to positively expect an answer to their prayers. This is quite unlike the farmer who prayed for rain during an unusually long period of drought. After prayer he went to the window and, looking out at the cloudless sky, muttered to his wife, "Just as I thought. No rain."

So, when you approach the Bible to read and study expect something wonderful to happen. Believe that whenever you open the Bible to study, God has a special blessing for you. Some encounters with the Word of God will be more dramatic than others. Nevertheless, spiritual truth designed to meet human needs awaits the Christian who approaches the Bible with an attitude of expectancy.

This truth takes on new meaning for believers as they realize God is pleased when they practice it in their personal lives. It honors God when His followers believe His promises and expect a blessing from fellowship in the Word.

Reverently

One current trend in society is increased informality in social situations. Manner of dress, conversational styles, and cultural patterns all blend themselves into informal life-styles. There is much good to be said of this trend. People feel more at ease when they are not burdened with the pressure and uncertainty of coping with intricate formal customs.

The impact of these changing life-styles is being felt in all areas of society, including the Church. The confrontation of an older value system with an emerging new one sometimes creates problems for church leaders.

Amid the social upheaval and change occurring in society, some customs should maintain a timeless quality. One of these is reverence for God and His Word.

The English word *reverence* has several shades of meaning. Most of them, however, include the concepts expressed in the words *awe, honor,* and *respect.* The Bible, being the revelation of God to man, deserves reverence in its highest form. The prophet Isaiah gave a reason for this when he declared: "The grass withereth, the flower fadeth: but the word of our God shall stand for ever" (Isaiah 40:8). A treasure as eternal and precious as the Bible should evoke from every Christian a deep sense of reverence and appreciation.

Prevalent in society today is a subtle attempt to lower the Bible from the lofty position it has held in the history of man. Believers should be alerted to this condition. When we give the Scriptures their rightful place in the home, the church, the nation, and the individual's life there will be untold spiritual blessings.

In Old Testament times the Scriptures were highly respected even though they were not available for everyone to read. The art of printing multiple copies was not developed until much later in history. Copying the Scriptures by hand was a tedious undertaking; therefore, completed copies were precious.

The Book of Nehemiah dramatically illustrates the awe and respect the Israelites had for the Book of the Law. Under Nehemiah's leadership they had completed building the walls and gates of Jerusalem. In the process they had encountered great opposition. As the Israelites gathered to celebrate and worship, Ezra the scribe stood on a platform made of wood to read the Book of the Law. Nehemiah 8 describes the actions of the people as Ezra read. They stood when the Book was opened and even said, "Amen, Amen," with uplifted hands.

You will be a recipient of divine blessings as you honor and respect God's Word. So, approach it reverently, acknowledging its divine origin.

The Holy Spirit's Illumination

"But the natural man receiveth not the things of the Spirit of God: for they are foolishness unto him: neither can he know them, because they are spiritually discerned" (1 Corinthians 2:14). The human mind, although endowed with great brilliance, cannot comprehend spiritual truth through its own power.

Although the apostle Paul was referring primarily to the unregenerate person, there is an application for Christians. The student of the Bible who relies mainly on his own mental capacities to understand the things of God will experience disappointments. This does not stem from what he learns but from what he doesn't learn. Without the Spirit's help our growth in knowledge and understanding of spiritual things will be greatly limited.

Several young ministers were listening to an older minister speak at a conference. The men knew the speaker did not enjoy the benefits of a college education as they did. Although his formal educational background was meager in comparison to theirs, the breadth and scope of his knowledge of spiritual truth was surprising. They were deeply moved by the speaker's anointed ministry. In a later informal conversation with the speaker, they inquired about the secret of his outstanding ministry. Where did he get his unusual insight into Biblical truth? His reply was simple: "I read and study the Bible daily, and depend on the Holy Spirit to illuminate my mind so proper understanding will occur."

When you begin studying the Bible, then, acknowledge the limitations of your mind and invite the Holy Spirit to help you. This pleases God. It is His will for us to continually grow in the knowledge and understanding of the Scriptures. It will be a pleasant surprise for you to get new and exciting glimpses into Biblical truth when the Holy Spirit is invited to help.

The apostle John vividly describes this phase of the Holy Spirit's ministry: "Howbeit when he, the Spirit of truth, is come, he will guide you into all truth: for he shall not speak of himself; but whatsoever he shall hear, that shall he speak: and he will show you things to come" (John 16:13).

One word of caution as you proceed to study the Bible and invite the Holy Spirit to help. The truth He reveals should harmonize with that found in all other areas of the Word of God. Nothing in the Scriptures is contradictory. The interweaving and interrelatedness of Biblical truth is a most beautiful picture to behold.

Open-mindedness

Even the Holy Spirit cannot reveal truth to a mind that is closed. But what is meant by the term *open-mindedness?* Does it imply that a person is gullible? That he is ready to receive anything he hears or reads without any form of critical analysis or spiritual discernment?

There is a significant difference between maintaining an open mind toward truth and gullibility.

The open-minded attitude referred to in this chapter has these characteristics: It is receptive, searching, humble (acknowledges its limitations), discerning, and expectant.

The person who seeks to study the Bible and who approaches it with the right attitude is in for a delightful experience. He is about to step into a diamond mine richer than any found on earth. The gems of truth he finds will sparkle with eternal qualities.

One encouraging fact is that all people can be students of the Bible. It is not an exclusive club. God desires that all of His followers daily search the Scriptures. Those who are obedient will not only be recipients of spiritual blessings but will be afforded the privilege of sharing them with others. Approach the Bible, then, with the right attitude. Ask and expect the Holy Spirit to help you understand its truths. God will be greatly pleased as you honor His Word.

3

Where Did It Come From?

What is the Bible and where did it come from is a question men have asked for centuries. No book in history has aroused the feelings and challenged the intellect of man like the Bible. Each generation has produced outstanding pieces of literature. The information contained in many has significantly contributed to the advance of civilization. Authors in the fields of art, music, science, medicine, government, and religion have made invaluable contributions to man's cultural development. In fact, if scientists today did not have books containing man's accumulated knowledge, many modern inventions and discoveries would not have been possible.

The magnificent book called the Bible, however, has qualities that separate it from all others. It holds a unique place in the field of literature. For centuries it has had a major influence on the lives of human beings. So, then, what is the Bible and where did it come from?

Collection of Books

The Bible is a library in itself. The Old and New Testaments form a collection of 66 separate Books. These Books were written by about 40 different authors, in at least three languages, during a period of about 1,600 years.

A brief biographical survey of the authors makes it easier for most people to relate to the Bible. These men came from all walks of life and lived under varying circumstances. Most, like us today, were involved in the life of their community. Even though some of the prophets seemed eccentric, they interacted with others, not unlike people of today. One significant commonality was that each had made a personal commitment to serve God. Commitment was an essential quality in the lives of these men.

Few of them were professional writers. They came from backgrounds as diverse as: shepherds, kings, priests, fishermen, doctors, tax collectors, and soldiers. Some, like Moses and Paul, benefited from the best education afforded in their day. Others had little or no formal training. When God needed men, He chose those who were dedicated to His service and would yield to the voice of His Spirit.

Amazing Unity

One beautiful and amazing feature of these 66 Books is the complete unity of teaching. The Old Testament with 39 Books and the New Testament with 27 combine to form the Bible. Although the authors deal with diverse subjects, the unifying theme is the redemption of sinful man through a divinely appointed Saviour. This thread is woven through such varying fields of literature as history, poetry, biography, prophecies, and letters.

How could human beings from different generations, cultures, and backgrounds write books on a common theme without contradicting one another? They couldn't. As one reads books today by contemporary authors on a common subject and sees the contradictory viewpoints, he realizes how impossible it is. Then why is the Bible different?

Word of God

"All Scripture is given by inspiration of God" (2 Timothy 3:16). The reason for the uniqueness and unity of the Bible is because it is the inspired Word of God. It is not merely a record of man's quest for God as he has climbed the ladder of culture and civilization through the centuries. Neither is it a collection of writings describing man's view of God and his religious development. Rather, it records God's revelation of himself to man.

The Bible is the unfolding of God's truth to man so man might find a path back to God and a basis for fellowship with Him. The Bible alone is the Word of God. There is no other book, regardless of the many claims, that can be considered the Word of God. The Bible stands alone in history as God's revelation to man.

During Old and New Testament times, a revelation of God to man was usually referred to as the Word, the Word of the Lord, or the Word of God.

"In God will I praise his word: in the LORD will I praise his word" (Psalm 56:10).

"After these things the word of the LORD came unto Abram in a vision, saying, Fear not, Abram: I am thy shield, and thy exceeding great reward" (Genesis 15:1).

"But he said, Yea, rather, blessed are they that hear the word of God, and keep it" (Luke 11:28).

The term *word of God* is used frequently in the New Testament; therefore, Christians often refer to the Bible as the Word of God or the Scriptures. It can rightly be called the Word of God because it contains God's Word as He revealed it to man.

It's Inspired Too

Students of the Bible often refer to it as being inspired. Why? There is good reason for this, because the Scriptures themselves claim to be inspired by God. Perhaps like many, you are confused and wonder what the word *inspiration* actually means, especially when pertaining to the Bible. Specifically, then, what is meant by inspiration of the Scriptures? Inspiration is a special act of the Holy Spirit by which He guided the writers of Scripture, insuring that their words were free from error and omission and that they conveyed the thoughts the Holy Spirit desired.

The inspiration of the Bible means that its contents was communicated to the writers by the Holy Spirit. In the writing of the Scriptures we see a beautiful picture of how God used men in a special and unique way. Certainly He could have used other methods. Some wonder why God did not write the Bible in heaven and have the angels deliver it. But God knows best. He chose man, even though weak and prone to failure, to be the channel through which He would reveal himself to the world. What an indication of God's mercy and His desire to fellowship with us!

Still Human

The Bible refers to the Scriptures as being inspired. The authors were moved on or guided by the Holy Spirit when they wrote. Therefore, almost nothing is more important to evangelical Christians than the doctrine of the inspiration of the Holy Scriptures. Remove the belief of inspiration from the Bible and you have just another book.

The battle over inspiration and authority has continued to a greater or lesser degree over the span of history and it has not abated in modern times. On the contrary, this critical issue of inspiration is being discussed and challenged today as never before in the history of man. There are some vocal remnants left of modernism and higher criticism, but another subtle approach has developed. This approach accepts the Bible as inspired but seeks to weaken the concept by stating it to be less than God declared it to be. To make certain we understand the full meaning of inspiration let us consider several aspects of it.

Most evangelical scholars use the term *verbal* when discussing inspiration. It means that every word in the original manuscript was inspired by God. This does not mean that the writers were mere secretaries who took dictation from God. Each writer used words from his own vocabulary which the Holy Spirit approved and prompted him to use. Of the approximately 40 writers, no two were alike. The styles, personalities, and vocabularies differ but the message is God's; therefore, we see unity as the divine message is unfurled.

Plenary inspiration means the full inspiration of all Scripture. Not parts here and there but all Scripture from Genesis through Revelation is inspired by God. One thing is certain, you can trust and rely on the teachings contained in the Bible. It is God's revelation to you and to all of mankind.

The defense of the inspiration of the Scriptures is not made on the basis that it is the historic position of the Church, although this may be true. Our position is based on the testimony the Bible presents regarding its own inspiration. Other conclusive evidence is found in the fact that Christ accepted the Old Testament as the Word of God. Because God took great care to provide by inspiration an errorless record of His revelation in Old Testament times, it is certainly reasonable to believe He would have taken equal care to provide by inspiration an errorless account of the establishment of His church.

Final Authority

The word *authority* arouses a wide range of feelings in people. A spirit of rebellion against authority of any kind is prevalent in the world today. People who have embraced this philosophy refuse to acknowledge their dependence on powers outside of their own being. It is entirely different with Bible-believing Christians. We acknowledge the Scriptures as the ultimate and final authority in matters relating to our experiences with God and our life-styles.

The Bible is the authoritative Word of God. It is the expression of God's complete plan for our lives as individual Christians and the Church as a body. Ignorance of Biblical teaching inevitably leads to a lack of understanding God's plan for us. But Christians read the Bible with total confidence, knowing that every word and every teaching comes from God. No wonder believers have such delightful experiences reading and studying the Bible. We have the inerrant (the state of being free from error) and infallible (incapable of error) Word of God. The ministry of the Holy Spirit in illuminating our minds, teaching us, and helping us desire to obey God is available to every Christian.

For the Christian the Bible is the supreme court

from which there is no appeal. What the Scriptures declare on any given subject is final. As followers of Jesus Christ we should submit completely to the authority of the Bible. Is this too difficult? Not when you consider His innermost love for man. Through the Bible He provided a new and dependable medium of fellowship with those who would believe.

Who Wrote It?

Who wrote the Bible? The answer is twofold. The Holy Spirit is the Author and He employed human instruments to accomplish the work. This is not unusual. Throughout the span of history God has used men and women in marvelous ways to work out His eternal plan.

Three languages were used in writing the Scriptures: Hebrew, Aramaic, and Greek. Almost all of the Old Testament was written in Hebrew, with limited portions appearing in Aramaic. The New Testament was written in Greek.

Manuscript, What's That?

Each human author wrote as he was guided by the Holy Spirit. He wrote on whatever material was available in his day. Words could have been etched in stone or handwritten on parchment. The original handwritten copy as well as handwritten copies of the orginal work are called manuscripts. The actual writing of the Bible is veiled in obscurity.

It is a startling fact that there is not one known original manuscript of the Bible in the possession of any individual, church, or library. It would have been no problem for God to preserve them had He desired to do so. But, if they did exist, would they have become objects of worship? The Old and New Testament manuscripts available to us today are ancient copies of the originals. Versions are translations of these manuscripts. The scribes who copied them accepted them as inspired writings and were well-schooled in the importance of painstaking care to assure accuracy.

Today about 5,000 ancient New Testament manuscripts may be found in libraries all over the world. The better known ones include the Codex Sinaiticus (a magnificent parchment copy of the Greek Bible dating from the fourth century), the Vatican Manuscript, and the Alexandrian. A recent and very significant discovery was the Dead Sea Scrolls found in 1947. They include all of the Old Testament, except Esther, and date from the centuries just before and after the birth of Christ.

A valid and interesting question is how did the 66 Books of our English Bible come to be regarded and accepted as the Holy Scriptures? Did God collect, bind, and publish it in heaven and deliver it complete to man? No. He again chose to employ human instruments to accomplish His purpose.

Canon of Scripture?

Originally canon meant a "rule" or "measure." The Books of the canon are those that have been measured by a certain rule and as a result are included in the Bible. We should remember that many writings on religion existed in both Old and New Testament times.

The Old Testament canon was established before the time of Jesus. He and His disciples often referred to the "Scriptures," and thus implied that some writings were Scriptures and others were not. The inspired writings of the apostles were given immediate canonicity, not a gradual elevation to a place of authority. For example, Peter writes of Paul's epistles as being a part of the "Scriptures" (2 Peter 3:16). By A.D. 691, the full New Testament as we know it today was completed. So, God used human instruments to write, preserve, and compile the Books we call the Holy Bible.

What About the King James Version?

Many different English versions have been translated and published over the years. The most well-known and loved is the King James or Authorized Version. Completed in 1611, this masterpiece has been used by millions of Christians.

However, although the King James Version's literary excellencies made it superior, some of its words have fallen into disuse or lost their original meaning. Consequently, many new versions have been translated and published.

Although modern translations are helpful, the King James Version remains the most popular and best-loved translation. A committee of about 50 of the leading Hebrew and Greek scholars of the day began their task in 1607. In 2 years and 9 months their work was ready for the press and publishing was completed in 1611. The King James or Authorized Version is the last and the best of the English revisions of the Reformation period. Many versions have appeared since 1611, but none has taken the place of the King James.

4

Let's Read It

The magnificent Book of books called the Bible is the greatest treasure ever possessed by man. It is God's revelation of himself to us. In it we learn about the love, mercy, and goodness of God. Revealed in it also is the divine plan of salvation. It contains many profound truths, but the fundamental ones relating to man's sinful condition and God's promises are clear and understandable to all.

Its account of the beauties of Creation is an indication of the presence of the great Creator: "The heavens declare the glory of God; and the firmament showeth his handiwork" (Psalm 19:1). The Bible, then, is filled with the knowledge man historically has sought and longed for. He comes to the end of his search for truth when he sees the manifestation of God in the person of the Lord Jesus Christ as revealed in the Scriptures. But we must read the Bible to learn who God is, what He has done, what He is doing, and what He yet will do.

Read Daily

The society in which we live today is characterized by haste. People are in a hurry. Every activity we engage in seems to have a built-in time limit. How can a person find time to read the Bible daily?

Many Christian leaders are convinced that

time is not the major problem. Priorities, they emphasize, are the crucial issue. Each day has 24 hours and God has given us freedom to choose how we will use them. Sociologists say that usually a human being will choose minute by minute the item he considers of highest importance. As followers of Jesus Christ and citizens of heaven, fellowship in the Word should occupy a high position on our scale of values.

Love is a force that goes beyond the perimeter of duty. As Christians grow to love Bible reading it will rise to new heights on their priority list. No longer will it be a duty that is performed spasmodically or when there is nothing more important to do. Instead, there will be an eagerness to read the Word and an excitement caused by anticipation. The heart of the Christian who has learned to love God's Word will beat with a certain kind of excitement as he opens the Bible to read. His awareness that this Book contains an inexhaustible supply of spiritual treasure will be a powerful motivation to search its pages. Bible reading will become a cherished and spiritually uplifting event of the day.

Daily reading of the Word of God will supply the spiritual needs of the mind, the emotions, and the will.

Fortifies the Mind

Our minds need the influence of the Word of God every day. They are bombarded continuously by information and influences that are not conducive to Christian living. The effects of our materialistic and highly secularized society on the minds of Christians are often extremely negative. Unless there is a positive counteracting force the results are often devastating to the Christian's thinking patterns.

But we live in this kind of world and cannot isolate ourselves from these influences. Cheer up! *Daily fellowship in the Bible will fortify the mind against all negative influences of a worldly society.* The believer who begins each day by reading a portion of Scripture has established a positive mental pattern. He has declared his priorities to himself, to God, and to the forces of darkness that would seek to turn his thoughts astray.

But the human mind is so prone to forget! Divine truth from God's Word fades into dimness if it isn't renewed by daily reading. Christians today who follow the pattern set by the Psalmist will joyfully discover that their understanding of the Scriptures is growing. The Word hidden in their hearts and minds will be an effective implement of warfare in the battle against sin and evil. "But his delight is in the law of the LORD; and in his law doth he meditate day and night" (Psalm 1:2). Meditating in the Word will become a delightful experience for you also.

Reading the Bible will stir up the mind to remember the truths learned previously (2 Peter 3:1, 2). One plague that has affected the minds of men today is the tendency to fret and worry about problems. Even many young people who are offered the greatest opportunities in the history of mankind often find themselves caught in the grip of worry.

Christians, too, who live below their privileges sometimes permit themselves to become trapped by worry and anxiety. Again, the Christian who daily fortifies his mind by reading the Word of God and praying will be able to rise above this condition. He need not be a victim of worry and fear (Matthew

6:34; Philippians 4:7). Discipline and strength come to the mind through the Word (2 Timothy 1:7). Through reading the Bible we learn that our minds are enlightened (Ephesians 1:17, 18), transformed (Romans 12:1, 2), and renewed by the work of the Holy Spirit (Titus 3:5).

Many fine Christians today are aware of their human weaknesses and tendencies to be overcome by worldly temptation. They earnestly desire to live a consistent Christian life but all too often are overcome by temptation.

Look up and rejoice! The Bible has the answer: "Thy word have I hid in mine heart, that I might not sin against thee" (Psalm 119:11). When the human mind is daily nourished by truth from God's Word it will not easily fall prey to the attack of Satan or worldly temptation. The Word of God is a mighty fortress against sin, but Christians must consistently read the Word if they are to benefit from its influence. Even though our minds are prime targets for attacks of Satan, daily reading of the Bible will repel them and bring sure victory.

Helps the Emotions Too!

Another area of the Christian life where a tremendous struggle takes place is in the emotions. The Gospels and the writings of Paul describe this battle in detail.

Have you ever lost control of yourself and in anger said things that were unkind and perhaps even cruel? Later you were sorry and even asked forgiveness, but the damage was already done. Or maybe someone mistreated you or made unkind remarks about you. If so, how did you react? Do you live daily with bitterness in your heart toward someone?

Some Christians are plagued by a spirit of jealousy. They seem unable to control this emotion. Even though they love God and are willing to serve Him these emotions are constantly churning within causing unrest and tension. How often do we cry out from the very depths of our souls, "Lord, deliver me!" The emotions of anger, bitterness, jealousy, and hatred have a devastating spiritual and physical effect especially on those who harbor them.

What, then, is the answer? Emotional control can be the norm for every Christian, young or old, who yields his life to the mastery of the Word of God. The influence of the Holy Spirit and the Word will help the Christian to develop self-control. Only then will sinful emotions, such as anger, bitterness, and jealousy, be brought under control. They will be replaced by the fruit of the Spirit: love, joy, peace, contentment, and kindness.

This change will result in inner healing. No longer will there be outbursts of anger or inner churning of resentment or jealousy. All this has been changed by reading the Word of God and yielding to its power. "Put on therefore, as the elect of God, holy and beloved, bowels of mercies, kindness, humbleness of mind, meekness, long-suffering; forbearing one another, and forgiving one another, if any man have a quarrel against any: even as Christ forgave you, so also do ye" (Colossians 3:12, 13). This condition can become a reality in your life by yielding to the mastery of the Word and prayer.

Strengthening the Will

The real key to consistent Christian living lies in a will that is yielded to the power of the Word and the Holy Spirit. Reading the Bible imparts strength to our will which is the part of us that regulates our choices. If the will is weak we shall drift; if it has been strengthened by the power of the Word of God and the Holy Spirit, we shall overcome. "I have written unto you, young men, because ye are strong, and the word of God abideth in you, and ye have overcome the wicked one" (1 John 2:14). A very important spiritual law to remember is when the will is daily yielded to God, the mind and emotions will follow along in obedience.

Read Prayerfully

Prayer makes reading the Scriptures a delightful experience. When a season of prayer accompanies Bible reading untold spiritual blessings accrue to the believer. It helps to prepare the heart and mind to properly assimilate the truth. Many Old Testament saints were aware of this. "For Ezra had prepared his heart to seek the law of the LORD" (Ezra 7:10).

When we approach God's Word with an attitude of prayer and worship, we no longer face it as a task. Prayer warms the heart and conditions the mind to receive the instruction, correction, and spiritual food that God has prepared. There is no rebelling, no rationalizing, but rather an eager acceptance and personal application of the truth.

The Christian who follows this pattern will experience a newfound joy and peace. His spiritual life will not be anemic. He will discover a source of power that will enable him to withstand all attempts of the evil one to destroy him. Instead of just holding on or losing ground spiritually, he will be able to launch an aggressive warfare, invading the enemy's territory, and, as Paul contends, through God destroying the enemy's strongholds (2 Corinthians 10:4).

Hundreds of years before Christ, the Psalmist graphically described this kind of believer: "And he shall be like a tree planted by the rivers of water, that bringeth forth his fruit in his season; his leaf also shall not wither; and whatsoever he doeth shall prosper" (Psalm 1:3).

This is a spiritual formula that never fails. Prayerfully reading the Bible every day will bring growth in grace and in the knowledge of God. Dedicated Christians who are growing can be used by God to fulfill His purpose here on earth. Translating the words of the Psalmist into today's expressions, these believers are like trees planted by the waters, because their lives are continuously bearing spiritual fruit. From their lives will flow blessings to a dying world that is reaching for help.

Read Systematically

A Sunday school college class was engaged in a lively discussion. Everyone was so involved they hardly noticed the secretary as she opened the door to get the attendance record. "How should a young person read the Bible?" asked one of the students. After several minutes of discussion one bright young lady offered her answer. "Because we are instructed in the Bible to search the Scriptures, we should make certain to read all of them," she commented.

We readily agree. Systematically reading all the Word of God will produce definite spiritual growth in the lives of Christians. In fact, no other activity can take the place of systematic Bible reading. Prayer is an indispensable element in spiritual growth, but it does not take the place of consistently searching the Scriptures.

When Jesus was tempted in the wilderness His

answer to the devil was most significant. It has definite implications for the Christian and his Bible reading. "But he answered and said, It is written, Man shall not live by bread alone, but by every word that proceedeth out of the mouth of God" (Matthew 4:4). Undoubtedly, He meant that every word God speaks should command the attention of man, and this includes all of the Bible.

What is meant by systematic Bible reading? First, it is wise to set aside a definite time each day to let God speak to us from His Word. Following this pattern will require definite self-discipline. But don't we assign specific time slots during the day to other activities of life? Housewives prepare meals at given times of the day depending on their family's schedule. Young people attend school and classes at specified times. Businesses and industry in most communities announce a time schedule for conducting their operations. Churches also are careful to announce the time schedule for services and other functions. When we realize the extent to which the activities of our daily lives are scheduled, is it asking too much of ourselves to include Bible reading?

Reading the whole Bible is implied in systematic Bible reading. Many Christians find great joy in reading through the entire Word of God every year. This can be done by reading two chapters in the Old Testament and one in the New Testament every weekday, and three in the Old and two in the New on Sundays. On the other hand, if one chapter is read each day it will take about 3 years to read through the Bible.

Many Christian leaders recommend reading an Old Testament and a New Testament passage each day. Whatever method of Bible reading is chosen, let it be systematic.

With Enjoyment

Recently a star professional football player was being interviewed after his team had won a hard-fought game. He stood before the TV camera looking weary, his uniform covered with dirt. But he was happy. After discussing the dangers that football players face during a game, the commentator asked him a piercing question: "Why do you play this game?" With a smile on his face and without hesitation he answered, "Because I enjoy playing football."

Perhaps many of us are not football fans but we can appreciate this player's answer. It is the key to successful participation in most events of life. When we enjoy an activity the probability of benefiting from involvement is greatly increased.

This is especially true of Bible reading and study. "Thy testimonies also are my delight, and my counselors" (Psalm 119:24). Also, "I rejoice at thy word, as one that findeth great spoil" (v. 162). Christians who have learned to appreciate the Word of God will also learn to enjoy it.

Like some other Christians, you may have a question in your mind at this point. Along with them you earnestly desire to enjoy reading the Bible but how can a Christian develop this attitude? What is the secret some have found that makes Bible reading such an enjoyable experience for them? There are, in fact, three secrets.

First, to enjoy Bible reading one must develop a keen appreciation for the Bible itself. Watch a musician perform. Many enjoy his music but only those with an appreciation for the difficulties of performance, the discipline of study and practice, and the use of technique enjoy it to the fullest.

There is much about the Bible that commands the attention of men. Its literary excellence, historical accuracy, and, most important, its message make it the Book among books. No other book records the revelation of almighty God and His message of redemption for mankind.

Second, to enjoy reading the Word of God it must be read with understanding. A definite commitment of one's life to God is the first step. When this is followed by a growing faith in the Holy Spirit's help, the door to understanding the Scriptures is wide open. Enjoyment will increase as understanding grows.

Third, to enjoy Bible reading there must be personal involvement. It has a message that affects the intellect, the emotions, the will, and the very soul of man. Obeying its message will bring a cleansing from sin and sometimes radical changes in one's life-style. As you learn to make a personal application of Biblical truth, you will grow in the enjoyment of reading it.

So, let's read it!

5

Study the Bible—How?

Dwight L. Moody declared: "I never saw a useful Christian who was not a student of the Bible. If a man neglects his Bible, he may pray and ask God to use him in His work, but God cannot make much use of him; for there is not much for the Holy Spirit to work upon. We must have the Word itself, which is sharper than any two-edged sword."

A most encouraging fact is that one does not need to be a great scholar to study the Bible. Many great Bible lovers and students possess few natural talents but are constantly gleaning new insights and truths.

What an exciting time in history to be living! There is a rising tide of interest in Bible study nationwide and perhaps even around the world. Study groups are being formed in high schools, factories, shops, businesses, and among professional groups.

A young high school junior enjoyed private Bible study so much he decided to start a sharing time during one of his free periods at school. After securing permission from the school administration he quietly spread the word among the students about his plan. To his amazement and great joy the room was filled with students carrying Bibles at the very first session. Catholics, Protestants, and students with no church affiliation crowded into the room until the group had to spread into several units. Only eternity will reveal the fruits of this young man's labors. Meanwhile, he continues to share with others the spiritual truths gleaned from personal study of the Word.

It's a Real Battle

For many people, personal Bible study is a real battle. The distractions are many. Phone calls, visitors, emergencies, and even routine responsibilities often encroach on the time set aside for Bible study. How easy it is to take the line of least resistance.

Christians need to carefully analyze how they use their time. There is something definitely wrong in the life of a believer when he goes days without spending time in the Word. Unwise use of time is one of the greatest deterrents to spiritual growth and maturity.

Then, too, the Christian must always keep in mind that he is engaged in spiritual warfare: "For we wrestle not against flesh and blood, but against principalities, against powers, against the rulers of the darkness of this world, against spiritual wickedness in high places" (Ephesians 6:12). These wicked forces work against the Christian. Although our knowledge of them is limited to what the Scriptures reveal, we know their design is to spread evil on earth. Satan will use every device possible to keep us from studying the Word of God. He is aware of its great power and authority. Knowing this, we should let nothing hinder us from studying the Scriptures.

More Than a Book

The Bible is more than a book—it is the eternal Word of God. Because it is different from all other books, searching its pages requires a different approach. Works of science challenge the intellect, philosophy demands the use of reason, while art and music appeal to our aesthetic senses. Bible study invites the use of these faculties but also requires another dimension. Human intellect and reason at their finest are inadequate to discern and understand spiritual truth.

This new dimension that makes the difference is the teaching ministry of the Holy Spirit. His assistance in learning and comprehending Biblical truth is available to all believers regardless of their station in life. When a Christian yields his intellect and reasoning power to the influence of the Holy Spirit there is no limit to the depth and breadth of spiritual understanding he may achieve. This process of learning and gaining new insights into God's Word continues on throughout one's entire life. And perhaps there is much truth in the words of a veteran minister when he declared: "Eternity holds much for the Christian. There will be a continual revelation of the person, majesty, and beauty of God."

The apostle John in simple terms instructs us about the teaching ministry of the Holy Spirit: "He will honor and glorify Me, because He will take of (receive, draw upon) what is Mine and will reveal (declare, disclose, transmit) it to you. Everything that the Father has is Mine. That is what I meant when I said that He will take the things that are Mine and will reveal (declare, disclose, transmit) them to you" (John 16:14, 15, *The Amplified Bible*).

He Can't Do Our Part

Even though the ministry of the Holy Spirit is essential to understanding the Bible, He cannot do our part. He can only assist us when we put forth the effort required of us. People who wait for a new revelation without studying the Scriptures will be disappointed.

Perhaps, like many others, you would like to ask a very significant question at this point: "What steps do I need to take in studying the Bible so the Holy Spirit can help me gain a deeper and clearer understanding of spiritual truths found in the Bible?" This is a good question and deserves an answer. Earnest Christians everywhere desire to let the Holy Spirit illuminate their minds as they study the Word. Then, you inquire, "What should I do?" The Book of Proverbs goes a long way in answering this question. A careful analysis of 2:1-5 will help answer your question.

Receive My Words (Proverbs 2:1)

We must approach the Bible with an absolute conviction that it is God's Word through which He speaks to us. There can be no hidden doubts. We do not need to prove the Bible first and then accept it; we accept it and let it prove itself. Those who doubt the authority of God's Word cannot expect to receive anything from the Lord (James 1:6, 7).

But those who receive the Word of God into their hearts without doubting can expect to receive strength and blessing for every need in life.

There are many people who consider it a sign of intelligence to express doubt. And some situations in life do demand careful evaluation. But the Bible-loving Christian realizes that God in His wisdom did not choose to give us answers to all questions. Where do we learn this fact? In the Word of God, of course! "The secret things belong unto the LORD our God:

46

but things which are revealed belong unto us and to our children for ever, that we may do all the words of this law" (Deuteronomy 29:29).

Because the Bible is God's infallible Word, you can read it, believe it, and receive it. As you make a personal application to your own life the awareness of walking in God's will begins to grow. The consciousness of pleasing God by walking daily in the light of His Word should be the normal experience of every Christian. Let your mind become filled with the knowledge of the Scriptures and understanding will come.

Let's Live It

After we have received God's words we must determine to obey them. It does little good for the mind to be conscious of what God requires if the will and heart are not prepared to obey. But, you ask: "How can I bring my life up to the standards set in the Bible?" You can't! Surprised? Our Heavenly Father did not plan for you to accomplish it by yourself. He is more aware of our human weaknesses and tendencies to failure than we are.

Then, what shall we do? Again, look to the Bible for the answer: "That ye might walk worthy of the Lord unto all pleasing, being fruitful in every good work, and increasing in the knowledge of God; strengthened with all might, according to his glorious power, unto all patience and long-suffering with joyfulness" (Colossians 1:10, 11).

Isn't that great! It is just what we would expect from our gracious Heavenly Father. He not only challenges us to adjust our life-styles to meet the standards set in the Bible, but promises to strengthen us with His glorious power. God will help us to translate the Word into our daily patterns of living.

Bible study coupled with a determination to obey will revolutionize a life. This is especially true as we invite and accept God's help. His mighty power working within not only creates in us a desire to obey but strengthens our will, making obedience possible. What a marvelous transformation occurs in the lives of Christians who study the Scriptures with a heart to obey. Hate, envy, jealousy, and bitterness vanish away and are replaced by love, compassion, and kindness. In light of this, the words of Paul take on new meaning: "Therefore if any man be in Christ, he is a new creature: old things are passed away; behold, all things are become new" (2 Corinthians 5:17).

Why Not Listen? (Proverbs 2:2)

Serious Bible study involves listening. What the Scriptures have to say is certainly worth listening to. A most critical principle of Bible study is to learn to read intelligently. But even more important, we need the illumination of the Holy Spirit. As we listen to His voice, He will make the teachings of the Word of God clear to our understanding.

Centuries before Christ, the Psalmist stated this principle effectively: "Give ear, O my people, to my law: incline your ears to the words of my mouth" (Psalm 78:1). So, Bible study without inclining the ear to listen will not be spiritually productive.

Going through the mechanics of study does not in itself constitute or assure learning. A Christian teacher was alarmed because her students consistently scored low on achievement tests. She proceeded to investigate. The students seemed to be interested. Most of them completed their assignments. Nevertheless, they were not learning as expected. After a lengthy investigation involving detailed examinations the teacher found that many of the students had failed to develop adequate listening skills.

Many Christians too read the Bible faithfully but are disappointed with the degree of progress they make in spiritual understanding. Is it possible that Christians who are aware of this problem in their lives have not sufficiently developed the habit of listening to the Holy Spirit so He can make the Word of God live in their hearts and minds? Your daily Bible study will be revolutionized as you open your life to the power and influence of the precious Spirit of God.

Prepare Your Heart (Proverbs 2:2)

"Apply thine heart to understanding" (Proverbs 2:2). These are the words of Solomon to whom God imparted an unusual degree of wisdom. Searching and preparing one's heart is an essential phase of Bible study. Without it the person may not be inclined to accept the truth the Holy Spirit wants to teach him. Unless the heart is prepared, we are likely to miss the truths of the Word of God.

It is interesting to note that different men in the Bible referred to heart preparation as an essential element to close fellowship with God. The Psalmist prayed: "Search me, O God, and know my heart: try me, and know my thoughts: and see if there be any wicked way in me" (Psalm 139:23, 24).

In light of this, at least two critical questions arise in our minds: "What does the Bible mean when it speaks of the heart?" And: "How can we prepare our hearts to receive God's Word?" These questions are a challenge but they deserve consideration.

Just what does the Bible mean when it refers to the heart? In the Bible the word *heart* is used in three major ways. The first two ways are for the physical heart and the center or inner part of a thing. These two are not important to our discussion. The third way the term *heart* is used in the Bible is significant. It refers to the inner seat of life and includes the soul, spirit, mind, understanding, and emotional life of man. Merrill F. Unger defines it similarly but in different terms. According to him, the heart is the center of the rational-spiritual nature of man.

Well, then, now that we know what the heart is, how can we prepare it to receive God's Word? First, we must have a willing heart (Exodus 35:5). Willing to read and listen to the voice of the Holy Spirit. Willing also to pray and to make adjustments in our life-style as the Spirit through the Word reveals deficiencies.

A young college student was praying at the altar after the Sunday night service. She felt deeply impressed to give more time to prayer. Although she led a busy life with school responsibilities, God had given her a special burden to pray for her classmates. She was very popular on the campus and had many friends. As she knelt in prayer the thought kept recurring to her. She asked herself what activities she could give up in order to pray more. Then she asked herself: "Do I have a heart that is willing to read the Bible and pray?"

Second, as Daniel did, we must purpose in our hearts to serve God (Daniel 1:8). On this occasion Daniel purposed or determined in his heart to take the course of action that would bring glory to God even though it meant sacrifice for him. We must determine in our hearts that nothing will hinder us from reading and receiving the Word of God.

Third, Paul tells the Roman Christians they have obeyed God from their hearts (Romans 6:17). In preparing for Bible study, heart obedience is necessary if we are to learn the spiritual lessons God has for us. Heart obedience implies more than mental assent; it involves the total spiritual nature of man. This kind of Christian delights in obeying God by fellowship in the Word and in prayer.

Finally, Paul, in writing to young Timothy, refers to love that comes from the heart (1 Timothy 1:5). There is no stronger motivation to read and obey the Scriptures than love. Christians who love God and His Word from the heart have found the secret to joyful, exciting Bible study.

Share It With Others

A family was vacationing in the Rocky Mountains. They had traveled for several days and decided to camp that night in Utah. The park where they were staying was located in the mountains by a beautiful lake. The scenery was magnificent. While they were eating supper and admiring the fantastic natural beauty, a park ranger stopped to visit for a few minutes. During the conversation he suggested that after supper they take a walk on a trail by the lake shore. "As the sun sets," he commented, "you will be in a position to see one of the most beautiful views on earth." After he left, the 16-year-old daughter exclaimed, "Hurry, Dad and Mom, we don't have much time until the sun goes down."

But everyone else in the family was too tired to walk that far so she decided to go alone. The sun had disappeared behind the mountains and dark

51

shadows were being cast over the area when she returned. She ran to her mother breathlessly and with excitement in her voice cried, "Mother, it was the most gorgeous sight I have ever seen. I just wish the rest of you could have been there to share that beautiful view with me."

How true this is of every meaningful experience we have. The joy is greatly increased when we can share it with others.

This is especially so of Biblical truth. What we learn in Bible study is reinforced in our own lives when we share it with others. The Bible itself teaches this: "And the things that thou hast heard of me among many witnesses, the same commit thou to faithful men, who shall be able to teach others also" (2 Timothy 2:2). So, the more you share the Word of God with others, the greater will be your joy. The spiritual benefits gained from sharing cannot be calculated by the human mind.

6

Tooling up for Bible Study

Tools. What would we do without them? Have you ever seriously considered this question? To successfully complete most tasks in life requires the use of some kind of tools. Highly sophisticated ones are needed for some work while the common lead pencil is adequate for others.

A farmer has tools of every description. How interesting it is just to view them. Medical doctors, dentists, students, teachers, factory workers, and people employed in any kind of work need tools. Imagine if you can an auto mechanic, a sales clerk, or a housewife attempting to perform their tasks without the necessary tools. Work would slow down immeasurably. Even if they improvised, the quantity and quality of work completed would be minimal at best.

What would students do without tools? Pencils, paper, and books of all descriptions are essential. These are tools. They contribute significantly to students' investigative efforts.

Students of the Bible are not exceptions. They too need very accurately developed tools when studying the Word of God. Fortunately, Christian scholars have developed an exceptionally fine array of tools that are usable by any person desiring to study the Scriptures.

A Favorite Tool

One afternoon a high school class visited a local dairy farm where the owner took them on a tour. He explained each operation as the students listened with amazement and interest. The tour culminated with a visit to the machine shop. After demonstrating and explaining how the various implements were used, he opened a chest and picked up an old wrench. As the students looked with wonder at it the farmer affectionately said: "This is my favorite tool; it always seems to work. I use it often."

The most important tool to use in studying the Bible is the Bible itself. Many people read a lot of books about the Bible. They are well-versed when it comes to factual information about it but know very little of what the Bible itself says. The Bible should be our favorite and most frequently used tool. We should be thoroughly familiar with its contents.

Bring the Parchments

The apostle Paul valued the Scriptures very highly. He had studied them for a number of years and was well aware of their power and authority. They were among his most treasured belongings: "The cloak that I left at Troas with Carpus, when thou comest, bring with thee, and the books, but especially the parchments" (2 Timothy 4:13). This great apostle set a fine example for Christians. The Scriptures were of prime importance to him.

When you purchase a Bible for study, one important feature is print size. Many people who are anxious to read and learn from the Word of God purchase one with such fine print that reading is difficult. Why invest in a Bible with print so small that it discourages anything more than a brief and casual reading?

It will make reading and studying more enjoyable and productive if you select a Bible with large enough print to make reading easy.

Another feature your study Bible should have is good quality paper. It would be well to choose one with paper suitable for marking. Many students consider this a high priority. Making notations and underlining key verses is critical to highlighting significant portions. If the paper is too thin, marking with colored pens or pencils often distorts print on the other side of the page.

Every student will want a King James Version. It is unsurpassed for its beauty of expression in the English language. Because this version is widely accepted in the Christian world, it is important to become thoroughly familiar with it before turning to other modern translations.

Translation—What's That?

Bible students often refer to different translations or versions. Sometimes this is confusing to persons who are new to the field of Bible study. A *translation* is simply the rendering from one language into another of any piece of literature. Historically, many different men or groups of men have translated the Scriptures from the original languages into another language such as English. Sometimes too the Bible has been translated from a language it was not originally written in into another language. The results of both are called translations.

But what is a version? Technically a version is a translation of a literary text only from the original language. But over the years the usage has changed and the meaning has been broadened. Today a *version* simply means any translation of the Bible or a part of it. An amplified translation is a Bible that has some commentary or explanations.

A Paraphrase?

As a student of the Scriptures your search for tools will inevitably lead you to Bibles called *paraphrases*. According to the *Wycliffe Bible Encyclopedia,* a paraphrase is a free, loose translation. It is a restatement of sentences, passages, or words that retains the original concept, but attempts to express the meaning more clearly or intelligibly to the reader. Some paraphrases of the Bible have allowed more leeway to the translator. Although translations may be more accurate, most paraphrases are interesting and enlightening.

One way to use a paraphrase is to compare a verse or passage in the King James Version with the same verse in a paraphrase. An example of this is the following comparison using 1 Corinthians 1:18:

> For the preaching of the cross is to them that perish, foolishness; but unto us which are saved, it is the power of God (KJV).

> I know very well how foolish it sounds to those who are lost, when they hear that Jesus died to save them. But we who are saved recognize this message as the very power of God *(The Living Bible).*

A paraphrase, like other tools, should be used in connection with other translations.

Which One for Me?

All widely accepted translations or versions have some commonalities and some differences. The major commonality, of course, is that the message is essentially the same. In careful translations the message is identical although it may be expressed in different terms.

Some of the primary characteristics that distinguish one Bible from another are: a concordance, maps, self-pronouncing, an index, footnotes, marginal notations, pictures, cross-referencing, a dictionary, charts, alternate renderings, print size, explanatory notes, and topical studies.

The major difference then in Bibles is in the combination of helps included by the publisher. It is impossible to recommend one that would meet the study needs of all students. Before purchasing a Bible you should compare these features. After you have carefully evaluated and compared the major versions, choose the one having the combination of helps best suited to your study habits.

A brief survey of the major translations widely used by Christians of all faiths is included in this chapter.

Scofield Reference Bible. This is a commonly used Bible that is well-known in the Christian world. The text is prominent in bold type with comments at the foot of the page and numerous synopses on various subjects. Some of the notes are excellent, while others are not acceptable because of a bias in interpretation. Unlike a number of Bibles, it is not self-pronouncing. A loose-leaf, wide-margin edition is available for those who wish to insert their own notes.

Thompson Chain Reference Bible. This thorough and helpful Bible has a host of notes in the margin and an excellent "Condensed Encyclopedia" divided into 4,129 topics. It also contains information on the principal English versions, an outlined analysis of each Book, a number of maps, a concordance, and an index. It has a good harmony of the four Gospels and several excellent charts.

Dixon Analytical Edition. This is another popular Bible used by Christians of all denominations. It is particularly helpful to students because of its topical studies, concordance, dictionary, outlines, and "outstanding facts of each Book" section. Its marginal notes are also a great help to students. References are footnoted below each verse and textual revisions are bracketed in the verses.

Time and space will permit us to mention only a few other Bibles you should evaluate before choosing one for study purposes. These are: *The New Testament: A New Translation* (Moffatt); *The New Testament in Modern Speech* (Weymouth); *The New English Bible;* and the *New Oxford Reference Bible.* Along with these are a number of modern paraphrases such as *The Living Bible* and *The New Testament in Modern English* (Phillips).

So—which Bible is for you? Evaluate and compare them. Ask yourself what combination of helps will be of greatest benefit in your studies. You are the only one who can make this choice. If it is made carefully and prayerfully you will be pleasantly surprised. A Bible with the proper size print, made of good quality materials, will last for many years. This kind of Bible coupled with the right features will make your study very delightful and productive.

Marginal Reference

One of the most common and useful tools used by students is the marginal-reference system found in many Bibles. Although at first it may appear highly complicated, a closer look will reveal its simplicity. You should thoroughly familiarize yourself with the marginal references in your Bible. The more often you use them in study the greater the benefits. They will soon become one of your favorite tools; and you will rarely study without using them.

Although references in a Bible may appear in various ways, the most common is the center reference column. Sometimes references are placed at the side column, under each verse, or at the bottom of the page. Where they are located is simply a matter of personal preference. The most important thing is to use them as often as possible. Only then will they contribute to meaningful and productive Bible study.

While using these references you can observe how they lead the reader from the first clear reference of truth to the last. Usually the first and last references are repeated each time. Thus, an entire series of scriptural references on a given subject is tied together to give the reader what the Bible has to say on it.

Another help, found in the margin of many reference Bibles, is an alternate rendering of a word, phrase, or verse. In some Bibles the margin also has general statistical information explaining such matters as money terms, weights, time, and figures of measurement.

What's a Concordance?

A concordance is a magnificent tool. Trying to study the Bible without one is like building a building without a hammer or preparing a cornfield for planting using a hand shovel. It is much easier and more productive to accomplish these tasks using the proper tools.

Simply stated, a concordance is an alphabetical

listing of key words used in the Bible along with all Scripture references where they are found. Therefore, when looking up a verse or passage of Scripture, if a student can recall any of several words in it he can easily find the passage by using a concordance. Consequently, it provides immediate access to any verse of Scripture if one remembers only a fragment of it.

The best known and most widely used are *Cruden's Unabridged Concordance*, Strong's *Exhaustive Concordance of the Bible*, and Young's *Analytical Concordance to the Bible*. Many Bible students prefer the last two because they are more complete.

For those who cannot afford a concordance it would be well to choose a Bible that contains one. Some Bibles have excellent concordances (usually found on the back pages).

Get a Bible Dictionary

A Bible dictionary is also a necessity. Most contain a wealth of material essential to understanding the meanings of words and terms employed by the men who wrote the Scriptures. Like any dictionary, it is an alphabetically arranged compilation of words and their definitions, but they are words with Biblical significance. Most dictionaries contain both common and proper nouns.

By using a dictionary the student gains a clearer understanding of difficult words and unfamiliar names of persons, places, and things. An exceptionally helpful feature of some Bible dictionaries is their use of pictures. A written definition coupled with a picture is an excellent description of an object.

Some of the more widely used Bible dictionaries are: *Davis' Dictionary of the Bible, Unger's Bible Dictionary, The New Bible Dictionary* by Douglas,

Smith's Dictionary of the Bible, and the new *Zondervan Pictorial Bible Dictionary* by Tenney.

Bible Atlas

A good Bible atlas is a marvelous tool for students. Most atlases contain maps, charts, or pictures of the ruins of ancient civilizations; interesting views of landforms important to Biblical happenings; and general information on Biblical geography, geology, and archaeology.

An atlas will help you to better visualize the setting of great events of Scripture. The missionary journeys of Paul, the ministry of Jesus (and later, of His disciples), as well as the journeys of Abraham take on enriched meaning when you use a Bible atlas.

Manners and Customs

Interesting and exciting books on Biblical manners and customs are available and will make a substantial contribution to Bible study. Most Christians are totally unfamiliar with the cultural patterns of people who live in Eastern countries. When the Holy Spirit moved on the men who wrote the Scriptures they expressed divine truth in language common to the people of their time and region. As did Jesus, they used everyday objects and customs to illustrate the message.

The purpose of books on Biblical culture is to help us visualize and understand some of these objects and customs. When this occurs our understanding of Biblical truth is greatly enhanced and enriched.

An illustration of this can be seen in the law of Moses: "When thou buildest a new house, then thou shalt make a battlement for thy roof, that thou bring not blood upon thine house, if any man fall from thence" (Deuteronomy 22:8). The Palestinian homes were built with flat roofs. Since the people of that day spent considerable time on their roofs, it was necessary to build a parapet or railing to guard against accidents. Knowledge of this custom will greatly assist the student in understanding this verse.

There are many other tools available to the Bible student. Commentaries, topical textbooks, Bible encyclopedias, and Bible handbooks are only a few.

As a student you should remember that Bibles with explanatory notes are convenient and helpful but should not take the place of the Word itself. All tools are good, but your focus should be on the Scripture itself.

7

How's Your Comprehension?

It was a busy morning. The fifth-grade class had just finished reading, and the students were excited about a field trip planned for the afternoon. They were going to visit a museum in a nearby city. At her desk sat the teacher with a bewildered look on her face. Something had happened during the reading session that was very disturbing.

Because school had been open for only 2 weeks the teacher didn't know the students very well. At the beginning of the reading session she had asked for a volunteer to read a short story orally to the class. A bright looking young lady raised her hand. At the same time several other students pointed to her claiming she was the best reader in the fifth grade.

She read the story flawlessly. Apparently she had learned her phonics well. A comprehension test followed the oral reading lesson. To the utter dismay of the teacher, the young lady understood almost nothing of what she had read.

Unfortunately, many Christians read the Word of God with very little understanding. This need not be. God intended for His people to read and understand the Scriptures. It is only as we understand Biblical truth that it can become an effective influence in our lives.

God and You

Before analyzing some of the principles relating to understanding, we must consider the two persons involved in the process, God and you. The Bible declares in many ways and in many places that God gives understanding to His people: "Make me to understand the way of thy precepts: so shall I talk of thy wondrous works" (Psalm 119:27).

A detailed knowledge of the mechanics of understanding will avail little unless there is a corresponding reliance on the illuminating power of the Holy Spirit. When Christians realize that God greatly desires them to understand Him and that He has made provision for it, the Bible takes on new meaning (Isaiah 43:10).

God was pleased when Solomon asked for understanding rather than wealth or long life (1 Kings 3:9, 10).

If we know God wants us to understand His Word, then what special qualifications do we need? Can any human being learn to know what God has revealed in the Scriptures? Yes, this is God's plan. The Word of God specifically declares what man must do if he is to understand what God has revealed.

Born of the Spirit

First, man must be born of the Spirit. Sin is the greatest barrier to understanding the teachings of Scripture. When this barrier is removed and fellowship with God restored, there is no limit to the depth or height one may reach in Biblical knowledge.

According to the Word of God, spiritual truth cannot be received by the human mind unaided by the Holy Spirit (1 Corinthians 2:14). But when Christ reigns in the heart of a person, the mind is open to receive Biblical truth. What a beautiful relationship the Christian has with God. Walking with Him, learning from Him, and receiving divine strength is his daily experience. Growing in knowledge and understanding, and sharing it with others, makes life worth living.

Desire and Seek

Second, the Christian should greatly desire and earnestly seek to understand the Word of God. It should be a high priority. God has promised to give us the desires of our heart, especially if they are in accordance with His will.

Seeking and desiring are important keys that help unlock the door to the mysteries of God. How often we read in the Bible that our Heavenly Father responds to those who earnestly seek Him. Yes, even to those who acknowledge their need for understanding (Proverbs 2:3-5).

Ask for It

Third, believers should earnestly pray that God will give them the spiritual insight needed to better understand the Scriptures. The Psalmist prayed: "Give me understanding, and I shall keep thy law; yea, I shall observe it with my whole heart" (Psalm 119:34).

Many lovely and well-meaning Christians become so deeply involved in the necessary activities of life that they fail to seek God for wisdom. A young man who had recently graduated from Bible college accepted the position of youth pastor in a growing church. The pastor of the church was considered highly successful by his peers and was loved by his congregation.

One afternoon the two ministers were visiting church members who lived several miles out in the country. As they drove along the highway the young man looked admiringly at the older minister and commented: "Pastor, it must be very rewarding to be so busy working for the Lord." After a few moments the pastor replied: "Yes, it's good to be active in the Lord's work. But we constantly face the danger of being so busy we neglect other crucial phases of life. We need to daily fellowship with God and seek Him for wisdom and understanding. Unless we seek God continually our efforts can become routine and meaningless."

Being Spirit-filled Helps

"But the Comforter, which is the Holy Ghost, whom the Father will send in my name, he shall teach you all things, and bring all things to your remembrance, whatsoever I have said unto you" (John 14:26). This is God's provision for every believer. The Holy Spirit will greatly assist you in understanding the Scriptures.

A lovely Christian lady had been saved for a number of years and was active in teaching Sunday school. She loved the Word of God. But at times she confessed to a lack of understanding when she read some of the deeper passages. At the invitation of a neighbor she began attending a ladies' prayer-and-praise group. There was something unusual and exciting about them. The worship and praise were beautiful and faith building. She listened intently as various members testified about having been baptized in the Holy Spirit. What a difference it seemed to have made in their lives! Now she too began praying that God would lead her into this glorious experience.

Then one day as she worshiped with her friends it happened. Her prayer was answered. She was filled with the Spirit. What a difference the Holy Spirit made in her life too! Among the many blessings resulting from her infilling was a greater love for the Word of God. It seemed to take on a new significance. Bible verses and passages came alive. The Holy Spirit helped her gain new insights that previously seemed hidden. It helps to be filled with the Spirit!

Do I Have to Study?

If I'm filled with the Holy Spirit why is it necessary to study? Won't the Spirit teach me? Yes, He will teach us but He can't learn for us. As we put forth the effort to search the Scriptures, the Holy Spirit will perform His illuminating and teaching ministry, so we will be able to rightly divide the word of truth (2 Timothy 2:15).

When a Christian follows the established principles of study he will discover that his efforts are productive and meaningful. His knowledge of the Bible will increase and the scope of his understanding will continually grow.

What Did He Say?

Usually it is important to first understand what the writer literally said. When this is firmly established the symbolic, prophetic, or applicational meanings can be determined more accurately.

To determine what the verse or passage literally means, we must carefully identify all persons, places, events, and objects. All words too should be carefully defined. For example, many Bible characters bear the same name. When we study a passage related to a given person, we should know which person is addressed. A Bible dictionary will be of great help because it lists every person and place mentioned in the Bible.

Define the Words Accurately

We cannot overemphasize the importance and necessity of accurately defining all words in a verse or passage. Bible interpreters who disregard the true meaning of words will have difficulty with interpretation.

Words in any given language change in meaning over the years. For this reason modern translations are helpful. Some study Bibles give the contemporary meaning of key words in the column reference area or in notes.

The Bible student should be aware that the King James Version, although widely accepted, was translated in 1611. Since then some English words have become either obsolete or have completely changed in meaning; for example: "For the mystery of iniquity doth already work: only he who now letteth will let, until he be taken out of the way" (2 Thessalonians 2:7). To the English-speaking world in 1611 this translation made sense. But what makes it so difficult for people today? The Word of God has not changed, and it never will.

Let us observe how the meaning of a common word has changed through the years, creating extreme difficulties for those who seek to understand. The word *let* meant "hinder" in 1611; today it means "permit" or "allow." Now read the verse again, but instead of the English word *let* insert *hinder*. It makes sense because we have more accurately defined a key word.

Verse, Chapter, Book, Bible

After all the words have been defined we are ready to determine what the verse means. But verses are fragmentary parts of a whole. Often a verse can be interpreted only by examining it within its context. Some verses don't make sense in isolation; but then, they were never intended to. Verse and chapter divisions were determined by man to make it easier to locate desired passages.

We need to remember that every verse is set in its own context which generally holds the key to the meaning of the verse or passage. Endeavoring to interpret isolated verses out of context sometimes can prove misleading.

We honor the Word of God when we take it as it stands and interpret each verse and each word in light of the entire passage. Each verse should be studied in light of the entire chapter, Book, or unit of particular truth. Promises and commands should be interpreted in light of their context.

To determine the literal meaning of a given passage there are five items the student should carefully observe. If this is conscientiously done, arriving at the meaning will not be too difficult.

First, determine who is speaking. It may be God, an angel, a saint, a sinner, a demon, or Satan. If the speaker is a man you should learn everything possible about him. What is his age, character, experience, and background? The more information you can gather about the speaker the more clearly you can understand his message.

Second, positively identify the person or group to whom the words are addressed. This is a most critical operation. Was the message meant exclusively for Israel, for Judah only, for all Old Testament people, for the Church, or for all people? Be careful not to generalize. This is a common mistake many Bible students make.

Third, determine as closely as possible the time when the message was spoken. Many good study Bibles give this information in the introduction to each Book or in the summary, usually found at the end of the Book.

Fourth, become familiar with the places referred to in a passage. Paul wrote to the Ephesians about the blessings in "heavenly places" (2:6). He also wrote to the Philippians: "For I have learned, in whatsoever state I am, therewith to be content" (4:11).

These passages become particularly meaningful when we bear in mind that both letters were written from prison and were sent to the Christians attending the churches in Philippi and Corinth. Reading about these two cities would greatly enrich your understanding of the messages sent to the Christians who lived there. What about the prison in Rome? How were prisoners treated by the Romans at that time? Under what conditions was Paul living when he wrote these letters? All of this information provides an excellent background.

Fifth, clearly determine the primary theme of the passage. If the passage is long, subtopics may be dealt with, but they usually relate to the main theme.

Now that we have defined all the words, identified who spoke, know the theme of the message, and determined who the message is for, understanding the literal meaning is not a mystery. If we have done our homework we are well on the way to greater insights. The Holy Spirit has something to work with.

Gaining Deeper Insights

After thoroughly understanding the literal meaning of a verse or passage the Bible student is in a position to search out the symbolic, prophetic, or applicational truths.

Many Biblical truths are like diamonds—they have several sides. Any slight movement of the gem will reveal a different glistening angle. To illustrate this process let us briefly study a rather familiar verse of Scripture: "And I will put enmity between thee and the woman, and between thy seed and her seed; it shall bruise thy head, and thou shalt bruise his heel" (Genesis 3:15).

What an interesting and profound verse! To properly and fully understand it we must view it in light of its context. But then, if we follow the simple rules discussed in this chapter, arriving at the intended meaning will not be such an impossible task.

Getting the Meaning

Let us assume the first steps have already been taken. We have defined all the words, identified the speaker and the ones spoken to, and determined the primary theme of the message. The critical question then confronts us: What is the literal meaning of this passage?

The verse in its context describes the historical conflict between serpents and human beings. There seems to be a natural enmity between them. Most people the world over are afraid of snakes and either avoid or kill them. The venom of poisonous species

71

can inflict great harm or even death upon man.

Unfortunately, some scholars stop at this point. They are satisfied with the literal meaning. Consequently, they deprive themselves of the rich prophetic, symbolic, and applicational meanings.

In figurative language we see the serpent representing Satan while the seed of the woman represents Christ or His people. The literal conflict between snakes and man pictures the spiritual battle between Christ and His followers and the devil. As snakes strike the vulnerable part of man, his heel, in turn man bruises the serpent's head.

The prophetic meaning is seen in the spiritual struggle between Christ, the seed of the woman, and the serpent or Satan. It was at the cross where Satan afflicted the body of Christ. There too Satan was dealt a deathblow. He was eternally defeated. Note here that to determine the prophetic meaning the Bible student must search beyond the immediate passage; in this case, to other Books, particularly the New Testament. Our treatment of this verse is not designed to be exhaustive but rather illustrative.

This leads to our final but highly significant point: the Bible itself is its best interpreter. It alone can qualify statements or words contained within its covers.

8

The Lamb With a Book?

A conscientious pastor had spent the afternoon
visiting new families living near the church. After
making several contacts he decided to make one last
stop before going home. One of his church members
had given him the name of a family that lived nearby.
Apparently this family was not in the habit of attending church and knew very little about God's Word.

After locating the house, he stopped and walked
up to the door. He rang the doorbell and waited a
moment, then the door opened slowly and a gentle-
man appeared. When the pastor introduced himself
he was invited in.

After exchanging the normal amenities, the pastor
explained God's plan of salvation to the man and his
wife. To his great joy, both of them knelt with him in
prayer. As he prepared to leave he encouraged them
to read their Bible and invited them to attend church
the next Sunday.

What a pleasant surprise it was for the pastor to see
their happy faces the following Sunday morning.
After church he could hardly wait to speak with
them. Just as the conversation was ending, the man
said: "Pastor, I have a question. We have been reading the Bible as you suggested. In Revelation we
read about the Lamb with a book. What does it
mean?"

We can't read and study the Bible long without becoming aware of its richness and beauty of language. From the beginning language has been man's primary means of communication. Can you imagine what the world would be like without it? God too has chosen to communicate with man by using language, both oral and written.

Bread of Life

Most languages make liberal use of figures of speech. Nearly all the ones used by a speaker or writer are derived from his cultural background and are vivid factors in the communication process. They give sparkle and life to what otherwise would be a mundane experience. The human instruments God used to write the Scriptures were no exception. Although the Holy Spirit guided the writers so they communicated God's exact message, they all used figurative language. It greatly helps the Bible student to know something about the cultural background of the writer. Was he a farmer? a shepherd? a fisherman? or perhaps a tentmaker?

Jesus the Master Teacher employed figures of speech to convey spiritual truth. For example, He declared: "I am the bread of life" (John 6:35). Why? Because He is to man spiritually what bread is to man physically.

A general knowledge of the more frequently used figures of speech found in the Bible will make reading more interesting and productive.

Jesus Used Parables

Parables are a most effective way to teach religious truth. They have been used for centuries by people the world over. Jesus made liberal use of parables during His earthly ministry. Usually His stories centered on situations common to his listeners. The themes focused on topics such as agriculture, marriage, family life, daily work, and the business world.

By the way, what is a parable? and why did Jesus use them frequently during His earthly ministry? A parable is a story that employs an ordinary circumstance of life to illustrate a spiritual truth. Jesus used them to bring out the deeper mysteries of the kingdom of God. Those who were interested in His teachings searched out the meanings, and in the process gleaned deeper truth hidden to the natural mind. Curiosity seekers and His enemies found it extremely difficult to understand the spiritual truth taught by the parable.

Jesus explained this to His disciples when they asked Him why He spoke in parables: "Therefore speak I to them in parables: because they seeing see not; and hearing they hear not, neither do they understand" (Matthew 13:13).

The parables of Jesus, then, are for those who firmly believe in His teachings. They are willing to search out the hidden truth through study and prayer.

Let's Look at a Parable

"Again, the kingdom of heaven is like unto a merchantman, seeking goodly pearls: who, when he had found one pearl of great price, went and sold all that he had, and bought it" (Matthew 13:45, 46).

Before we attempt to determine the meaning of this story let's review some principles essential to interpreting parables. Although space does not permit an exhaustive survey, the principles discussed should be helpful to the Bible student.

First, seek to understand the earthly details of the story as it was related by the speaker or writer. Try to visualize the unfolding of the account as told to the original hearers.

Second, try to ascertain as clearly as possible the attitude and spiritual condition of the original group to whom it was related.

Third, seek to understand the reason that prompted the speaker to use the parable. It should be remembered that Jesus did not always employ parables to teach others. He used a variety of methods.

Fourth, look for the literal details of the story. When this has been accomplished, pinpoint the central message.

Fifth, relate the central message to the spiritual emphasis of the speaker or writer.

In light of these principles, let's look at our parable, The Pearl of Great Price.

Although Jesus had been teaching a multitude of people, He was now speaking privately to the disciples. Even though they were growing in spiritual knowledge and maturity, there was much they did not understand. But they were keenly interested and were seeking to gain understanding, as evidenced by their request (Matthew 13:36).

Literal Details

The story centers on a merchant who was accustomed to buying and selling pearls. He made his living in this manner. Because of the nature of his operations he had acquired a keen sense of values. Although all pearls had some worth, he knew that a few possessed rare qualities that made them valuable above all others. He searched and bought and sold until he discovered one with a value exceeding all other pearls. When this occurred, he did not hesitate to act, but sold all he had and purchased it.

The central theme of the parable focuses on the attitude and behavior of the merchant. He persevered in his search until he found and acquired the most valued treasure, a pearl of highest quality.

Spiritual Meaning

Jesus likened the kingdom of heaven to the merchant and his value system. The incomparable value of the "new birth" and all the accompanying spiritual blessings are a major meaning of this story. Along with this is the encouragement to search out and acquire this spiritual treasure at any cost.

Parables are a rich source of hidden spiritual treasure. Study, perseverance, searching, and prayer are keys that help unlock the door to them. How interesting and exciting! The Bible is filled with sparkling treasures awaiting the reader—spiritual treasure that God intended to be your possession. Searching them out and sharing them with others is your privilege.

Typology, What's That?

Typology is a most interesting study. It is based on historical connections. In typology the interpreter finds a correspondence between a person, event, thing, or institution in the Old Testament and one in the New Testament. For our purposes we will compare aspects of the Old Testament with the New Testament, although there are instances of types and antitypes within one Testament only.

Types and Antitypes

But what is a type? and what is an antitype? A type

is a person, event, thing, or institution in Biblical history for which there is a later fulfillment. The Holy Spirit as the Author of Scripture placed within the type a prefiguration of what would later be identified as the antitype or the fulfillment. The antitype then is the person, event, thing, or institution appearing later that fulfills or corresponds to the type. We often say that Moses is a type of Christ. Thus Moses is the type and Christ is the antitype. It is only as the antitype is revealed that the fuller and deeper meaning of the type can be discerned.

It should be clearly stated and understood that typology exists because God is omniscient and He controls history. It is God who caused persons, events, things, and institutions to come into existence and to embody characteristics that would later be identified in the antitype.

Volumes have been written about typology. Some Bible students have made extreme and unwarranted use of types. But this does not detract from the beauty and reality revealed in them. Below are some Scripture passages that illustrate our point:

Type	*Antitype*
Moses	Christ (Acts 3:19-26).
Brazen Serpent	Christ (John 3:14)
Melchizedek	Christ (Hebrews 5:5-9)
Adam	Christ (Romans 5:12-21)
Flood	Baptism (1 Peter 3:20, 21)
Feasts of Israel	Aspects of Redemption (1 Corinthians 5:7)

To be productive the study of typology requires prayerful searching. The rewards will be many— new truths, deeper meanings, and fuller revelations are only a few.

Using Similes

A *simile* is a figure of speech in which two essentially unlike things are compared. The comparison is usually made by using the words *as* or *like*. Jesus made liberal use of similes in vivid descriptions. Fortunately they are relatively easy to understand. They require little research but rather prayerful concentration. It is critical in approaching a simile to clearly understand the two things being compared.

Most of the writers of Scripture made wide use of similes. They are excellent grammatical tools to bring out deeper meanings. Let us review some:

"For as the lightning cometh out of the east, and shineth even unto the west; so shall also the coming of the Son of man be" (Matthew 24:27). This is a vivid description of the second coming of Christ. The word *as* is employed to bring out the comparison of lightning flashing across the sky and the coming of Christ. The reader cannot help but be deeply impressed and affected by the dramatic events that will occur.

"Forbearing one another, and forgiving one another, if any man have a quarrel against any: even as Christ forgave you, so also do ye" (Colossians 3:13). Again the little word *as* plays a significant role in the verse. It is the Holy Spirit's way of asking us to be like Christ in our actions. The same divine love and compassion that motivated Christ should characterize our relationships with others. He set the example in forgiveness.

You Mean an Allegory?

Many different figures of speech were used by the writers of Scripture. Most of them have some commonalities. All, however, have differences and each contributes richly to the understanding of the Bible. An *allegory* is another figure of speech that students of the Bible should be acquainted with. But what is it? An allegory simply is a story designed to make several points of comparison with a real-life situation.

When a reader interprets an allegory there are several things he should bear in mind that will help him avoid erroneous interpretations.

First, he should take careful notice of the speaker and who the original hearers were. The message was for them; therefore, knowing something about them will help him understand the message.

Second, he should try to ascertain the reason the writer used the device. And, third, he should state clearly the points of comparison.

Let us consider a passage in which the writer uses allegory.

"I am the vine, ye are the branches. He that abideth in me, and I in him, the same bringeth forth much fruit; for without me ye can do nothing" (John 15:5). Jesus uses allegory here to teach His disciples very critical lessons. They needed to thoroughly understand the message. The major points of comparison are: the disciples (the branches) were dependent on the Father (the husbandman) and on Him (the vine) for their spiritual life and development. In summary, the three points of comparison are: God the Father (husbandman), Christ (vine), and the disciples (branches).

Why Use Symbols?

A symbol usually is an object that represents something else by association or resemblance. A symbol does not state its meaning directly but rather suggests it. Some Biblical writers used symbols to explain meanings. Sometimes, however, they only partially explained the symbol, or in some instances gave no explanation. In these cases, interpretation becomes a difficult undertaking. So the reader should attempt to learn as much as possible about the object in its cultural setting.

In simple terms, symbols often are material objects presented to convey spiritual lessons. They are numerous and can be found throughout both the Old and New Testaments.

The study of Biblical symbolism can yield a rich harvest of spiritual truth. Unfortunately, some students have taken unwarranted liberties when interpreting symbols. To avoid this error let us briefly consider some guidelines to follow when we seek the meaning of symbols.

Observe the characteristics of the symbol and try to discover why the writer used it. Usually this can be done by studying the context. Note how it relates to the first hearers. Then, build on the meaning derived from the symbol as it was used in its cultural setting and prayerfully seek to discern the correspondence between the symbol and that which it represents.

Interpreting Prophecy

Prophetic utterances for centuries have captured the interest of mankind, particularly Christians. Faulty interpretation, even by some evangelical scholars, has caused much misunderstanding.

Generally, Bible students recognize two aspects of prophecy, "foretelling" and "forthtelling." Foretelling is the prediction of future events. Forthtelling means exhortation, instruction, or reproof.

It is important to properly interpret prophetic passages. Many students find this difficult because they do not follow general rules for determining the meaning of prophecies. We will not burden you with a multitude of complex laws or rules, but will suggest several that should prove helpful.

First, make a careful analysis of the passage within its context. Determine the meanings of all words and learn as much as possible about the background of the prophet and the people to whom he spoke. Analyze the passage in light of the events that preceded it and those that followed.

Second, it is of special significance to identify clearly the people for whom the prophecy is intended.

Third, make certain you thoroughly understand the prophetic message.

Fourth, if it has been fulfilled, be able to correlate the prophecy with the fulfillment. Identify clearly the prophetic elements in the prophet's message with the corresponding ones in the fulfillment.

Fifth, when you don't understand do not try to force a solution. Remember, we don't know everything. And some prophetic messages still have an element of mystery to them. There are answers, but maybe we haven't discovered them all yet.

9

Taking a Panoramic View

"And the LORD spake unto Moses that selfsame day, saying, Get thee up into this mountain Abarim, unto mount Nebo, which is in the land of Moab, that is over against Jericho; and behold the land of Canaan, which I give unto the children of Israel for a possession" (Deuteronomy 32:48, 49).

His name was Moses. Following birth, life nearly came to an abrupt climax for him as he floated in a basket among the rushes on the Nile River. If only this infant could know what the succeeding years would bring. It would begin in a palace and end on Mount Nebo. There was to be a blend of victory, defeat, joy, sorrow, success, and failure.

God had mightily used Moses. Crossing the Red Sea and trekking through the Sinai Desert, Moses led this people. Sometimes they were hungry and thirsty, but God always met their needs, often miraculously. After a 40-year journey, they camped at the very door of Canaan, the promised land. A land God described as one flowing with milk and honey. Imagine the anticipation of Moses.

Panoramic View

Then God spoke. He told Moses to climb up Mount Abarim. There at the summit, Mount Nebo, he was able to capture a breathtaking view of Canaan. His eyes could scan the north and the south. Moses was able to get a beautiful panoramic view of the promised land before he died.

One good way to study the Bible is to get a broad overview. Scholars like to call it the synthetic approach to Bible study. As Moses stood on Mount Nebo and gazed at the broad expanse of Canaan, so the student can take a synthetic or panoramic look at the Bible.

When you employ this approach your goal should be to see the Bible as a whole. Seeing the broad scope of each Book, or the Bible as a whole, will greatly facilitate the study of individual passages. It will be much easier to determine the meaning of selected verses or passages after you have acquired this wider view.

Synthesis simply means the combining of separates to make a whole. When pertaining to book parts, it means consideration of the book as a whole. Or, as the chapter title suggests, getting a panoramic view of the Bible.

Although the division of individual Books into verses and chapters is convenient and helpful, it does have some disadvantages. If students are not careful they can create artificial breaks in subject matter by viewing individual passages. This is especially true if they fail to relate the bits of truth to the whole Book or theme.

Search the Scriptures

Under any conditions study is mentally and physically tiring. To successfully achieve learning goals, the student must be motivated. It is common knowledge that people who are highly motivated are more likely to achieve their objectives. If surveying the Bible is a high priority, students will more likely engage in productive learning activities.

But how can we become motivated? What action can we take to elevate Bible study to a position of high priority in our value system? One significant step all Christians can take is to inquire about what the Scriptures say. Because we acknowledge the Word of God as our supreme authority, let us read its message. "These were more noble than those in Thessalonica, in that they received the word with all readiness of mind, and searched the Scriptures daily, whether those things were so" (Acts 17:11).

The Berean Christians must have developed an unusual confidence and trust in the Scriptures. This passage indicates they not only received the Word readily but daily searched the Scriptures. Believers today could well follow their example in this regard.

When the Word itself commends those who search the Scriptures, it should be a powerful source of motivation to Christians. Searching is tedious. But the awareness of pleasing God should greatly encourage the student to persevere.

Now That We're Motivated

The teacher of a Bible class had introduced his students to the synthetic approach to studying the Scriptures. They became excited about it and could scarcely wait to begin. Getting an overview of the Bible had taken on a new significance to them. One very earnest student inquired, "Sir, we are eager to begin studying, but where do we start?"

To be highly motivated but lack the know-how can be a frustrating experience. So—where do we start in our quest to get a panoramic view of the Bible?

Reading and Rereading

Reading the Bible is necessary and profitable, but it is not enough. You must develop a workable plan to study it systematically. Without doubt, most Christians read a daily portion as a devotional exercise. This is commendable and spiritually beneficial. It is unfortunate, however, when a believer only reads selected passages but never reads through a Book consecutively. It is true one can open the Bible anywhere and find truth. Sometimes the Holy Spirit does meet a special need in this manner. But to get an overview of the Scriptures a different approach must be used.

The first step is to prayerfully select a Book. You don't need to start with Genesis or Matthew. In fact, you might be better off to choose a short Book until you have mastered the procedure. The following suggestions for reading will help you get started.

First, after selecting a Book (preferably a short one), read it through at one sitting. Don't worry if you don't understand everything. Read at your normal rate, neither too fast nor too slow. You are not searching for details as yet. That will come later.

Second, read the same Book through several times. It is not necessary for the reading to follow in close succession. However, for maximum effectiveness the time interval should not be too great.

Third, read it again prayerfully, asking the Holy Spirit to help you remember the major points. This is one function of the Spirit's ministry, to bring to our remembrance the words spoken by God (John 14:26).

Fourth, keep reading it until you have a broad view of its primary message.

The first readings of a Book may not leave much

of an impression, especially if the content is unfamiliar and difficult. But do not become discouraged; the meaning will take form with successive readings, because faithful, prayerful, and systematic reading will not be fruitless. Soon details will begin to take shape in your mind. Continuous and persistent reading of a Book will give you a familiarity with it and will greatly help you gain an overview.

Background Information

It will help you, when studying a specific Book of the Bible, to search out significant background information. Ideally, it should be done after selecting the Book but prior to the first reading. However, there is something to be said too for acquiring this information concurrently with the first reading. Whatever manner you choose, the information will contribute appreciably to your understanding of the Book.

What do we mean by background information? Learning about the author and about social, moral, and political conditions of the time is of great value. Why the Book was written along with the date and place are also helpful things to know.

Many of the widely accepted study Bibles contain this background information and more. Often it is condensed and summarized on one or two pages. This makes it convenient for students who do not have the time or reference books necessary to search out the information.

Getting the Central Theme

Although the individual Books of the Bible contain numerous truths and concepts, each has a major or central theme. Sometimes the theme is reflected in the title of the Book. Once you have identified it, try reducing it to one written sentence or less. If you can't, then express it in as few words as possible. One caution, do not sacrifice comprehensiveness for brevity.

What is a central theme? For our purposes it is simply the main idea of a given passage or Book around which other supportive information is built. For example, what is the main idea of the Book of Genesis? Although scholars express it in different terms, the major theme of Genesis is "beginnings." Creation and the beginning of life, death, sin, dispensations, covenants, human culture and institutions, and many other inventions of man are discussed. The first verse in the Bible gives us this theme: "In the beginning God created the heaven and the earth" (Genesis 1:1).

Once you have identified the central theme of a Book many details begin to fall into place. Each subsequent reading will open up whole new areas of knowledge and understanding. You will begin getting glimpses of the overall pattern of the Book. One suggestion before we leave this subject: it is extremely helpful while reading to relate information to the primary theme as often as possible. This will greatly facilitate memory. You will be pleasantly surprised to discover how much you are able to retain because you can see relationships.

Who Wants to Outline?

Outlining is not all that difficult. Your work will lead you to a broader view and a deeper understanding than merely reading or memorizing the work of some other person. We are not minimizing the effort of scholars who have labored diligently to give us helps for Bible study. They are most valuable and appreciated. But the effort and labor you invest in making your outline will make it more meaningful.

But how do I make a good outline? Simplicity and comprehensiveness are its primary characteristics. Below is a portion of a sample outline of Genesis. Needless to say it is very general, but it will illustrate how to get started.

Genesis

The Book of Beginnings (Central Theme)
I. Creation
   A. Heavens
   B. Earth
   C. Plants
   D. Animals
   E. Human Beings
II. The First Home (Garden of Eden)
III. The First Sin
   A. Serpent
   B. Eve
   C. Adam
IV. The First Children

It would be a simple matter to continue by adding to this outline such major points as: the patriarchs, the Flood, Abraham, Sodom and Gomorrah, Isaac, Jacob and Esau, and on through Genesis to the death of Joseph. Once the skeletal outline is completed you can proceed to the next step.

Learning Factual Content

The synthetic approach to Bible study does not involve expanded interpretation and detailed analysis. The primary concern is to view the broad scope covered by the Book. After getting a bird's-eye view and outlining the major points, we turn our attention to learning some of the factual content. For the learning process to be effective you should relate the content to your outline. Learning Biblical facts without relating them to the Book as a whole is usually not very meaningful or productive.

Our study moves from the Book, with its central theme and general outline, to focus on factual content. People, places, events, significant happenings, and spiritual concepts are some of the areas you will need to survey.

Amazing Unity

The Word of God is different from all other books. There are no contradictions. Each Book is a unified whole in itself. The 66 Books blend their themes together into a beautiful harmony.

How can 66 Books written by about 40 authors over a period of approximately 1,600 years have perfect unity? This is especially amazing when one realizes the broad range of subjects dealt with and the varied backgrounds of the human authors. The answer is simple, the Bible has perfect unity because it has one Author, the Holy Spirit. And He has the divine attribute of omniscience (all knowledge). Thus it was no great problem for the Holy Spirit, who knows all things, to inspire such diverse writings and still preserve unity.

One positive feature of the synthetic approach is that it helps the student to see this unity. The more Books of the Bible you apply this study method to, the more clearly you will see the unity of the entire Bible. Often a truth has different aspects, but when the Bible deals with these its message is not contradictory. All facets of the truth, when clearly viewed, form a beautiful pattern. Our Heavenly Father does all things well.

Observe the Relationships

Seeing relationships is one major result of taking a panoramic view of the Bible. Bible students who learn history, doctrine, commandments, poetry, and other factual content but fail to see their interrelationships are missing a highly significant phase of Bible knowledge. What do we mean by relationships? Where do we start and what do we look for?

A good starting point is to determine the central theme of the Bible as a whole. The new student will need to check reference material to acquire this information. Although it is expressed in varying terms, the Bible's central theme focuses on the redemption of sinful man through the divinely appointed Saviour.

Now as you take a panoramic view of individual Books, ask yourself how each relates to the Bible's central theme. For example, how does Genesis, the Book of beginnings, relate to this theme? or to Exodus? or to Romans?

Look too for the relationships between events, people, political institutions, prophecies, places, and teachings. Usually you will need to consciously look for relationships, but it is not unusual for the Bible to mention some in the normal flow of events. As an example: "For as in Adam all die, even so in Christ shall all be made alive" (1 Corinthians 15:22).

Note that some relationships are observable when the synthetic approach is used. Others are more easily seen when different methods of study are employed, such as those discussed in the next chapter.

10

Getting the Facts

The synthetic method of study gave us an overview of the Bible or of a particular Book. We made a general outline and were able to see how major themes were related. This could be called a global look.

Because the Bible is the Word of God it is essential that we get more than a global view. We need to learn its contents in detail so we can make correct interpretations and applications.

We need an approach to study that will help us gain factual information. The inductive or direct method of study meets this need. We carefully examine a particular passage so we can better understand its content, meaning, and application. We seek to discover what the author intended to say, to recognize what he meant, and then to receive the message into our lives. While the synthetic method affords a telescopic view, the inductive method gives a microscopic view.

As a student of the Bible you are not content with knowing the central theme of a Book but are interested in learning all the details. Yes, even the different shades of meaning found in many words. We fully believe what Jesus said about the significance of every word: "And the devil said unto him, If thou be the Son of God, command this stone that it be made bread. And Jesus answered him, saying, It is written, That man shall not live by bread alone, but by every word of God" (Luke 4:3, 4).

The inductive method of study involves three major operations: observation, interpretation, and application.

Let's Observe

Careful study of any book, object, or event requires observation. The word *observation* is simply defined but has broad implications. To observe means to see, inspect, or take note of something. In the scientific community it also includes careful analysis and measurement. As one step in the inductive method of Bible study, it suggests a careful analysis or scrutiny of a specific passage. A detailed examination is made to search out all the truths the author stated or implied.

The Bible is the Word of God revealed in written form. It can be considered a masterpiece of literature. But it is significantly different from other literary classics because it was inspired by God. The Holy Spirit directed each writer of Scripture to record only the things that needed to be said on a given subject. Each author was moved to write those words, facts, and concepts that would best accomplish the purpose of his Book. Therefore, to analyze or examine a given passage properly and to understand the intent and meaning of the author we must give attention to the details of the passage.

Every passage of Scripture contains a principal truth. In addition to the primary meaning, it may include other less obvious truths. Biblical truths are like diamonds, some are found easily while others are hidden and must be sought for diligently. Why does some truth yield only to earnest searching? We are not sure why the Holy Spirit caused the Scriptures to be recorded in a manner to challenge the student. But the Word itself declares: "If thou seekest her as silver, and searchest for her as for hid treasures; then shalt thou understand the fear of the LORD, and find the knowledge of God" (Proverbs 2:4, 5).

Careful Reading

For our purposes observation of a passage of Scripture begins with reading. The apostle Paul writes: "Give attendance to reading" (1 Timothy 4:13). Evidently God intended for reading to be an important step in Bible study. The student should read at his normal rate, focusing his attention on words, phrases, sentences, and concepts. The major goal of observation is to learn all the factual information inherent in the passage. You will find it necessary sometimes to stop reading and look up a word's meaning or locate places in a Bible atlas. It is important when you analyze a passage to look up information you don't understand.

Words Are Important

It is unlikely a student can know what a verse means until he thoroughly understands what it says. Thus it is essential to focus attention on key words. Often a single word in a given passage contains not only a definition but also a major concept.

A first-year Bible college student was in the habit of reading a designated number of chapters each day. He had systematically read through the Bible every year. His class was deeply involved in the study of 1 Corinthians. During one session a lively discussion developed and centered on the third chapter. The instructor asked: "What did the writer mean in verse 9 when he told the Corinthian Christians they were God's husbandry?"

The student replied: "I have read that word many times but do not know what it means." The class spent the remainder of the session analyzing and discussing the meaning of the word *husbandry* and its significance in Scripture.

Word studies often yield rich nuggets of truth. So in the observation process it is essential to properly define and analyze words. It is not a waste of time to search diligently for hidden meanings or for different shades of meaning. We are using the microscope, as it were, and carefully examining every detail of a passage including word meanings.

The Spirit Helps

Because we have already emphasized the ministry of the Holy Spirit in Bible study, it will be referred to here only briefly. Obscure passages, hidden meanings, and personal application become clearly understood as the illuminating power of the Holy Spirit becomes operative in the life of the believer.

The earnest student has many pleasant surprises awaiting him. It is amazing what the Holy Spirit reveals to those who prayerfully and carefully examine the Bible. With the Spirit's help, any Christian can apply the inductive method to Bible study and gain rich and meaningful insights.

History, Doctrine, or Narrative?

From a literary viewpoint the Bible is of unsurpassed beauty. Its writers employed all the techniques used by secular authors. It stands alone, above all literary classics. Within its Books the student will find biography, history, poetry, narratives, law, parables, dialogue, prophecy, and so on.

It is important for you to be aware of the literary form of the Book or passage you are investigating. If it is dialogue, who is speaking, what is he saying, and for what group is the message intended? Observation cannot yield maximum information if the student doesn't know that the form is important. Each literary form yields truth in its own unique manner. The student who is aware of this and seeks to broaden the scope of his understanding in this area will benefit in many ways.

Take Notes

Students vary considerably in their ability and need to take notes. It is an extremely valuable skill and can be learned and improved with practice.

An important phase of note taking is outlining. For the overview, general outlining of major points is sufficient. When we employ the inductive or analytical approach we must make a detailed outline. Listing all the subpoints is essential for a fuller understanding of any given passage. The central theme is related to all the detailed information contained in the Book or passage. So, take notes, make detailed outlines, and underline key words and verses in your Bible. Like a scientist, your observations should be systematically organized and recorded to facilitate memory and further learning.

Observing Relationships

A highly significant phase of the inductive method is being able to see relationships. Recognizing general relationships between people and events is required for the synthetic method, but the inductive approach requires observing finer and more detailed relationships. A word of caution: We don't seek to create relationships but only to find them.

For instance, Jesus expressed the relationship between faith and healing: "But Jesus turned him about, and when he saw her, he said, Daughter, be of good comfort; thy faith hath made thee whole. And the woman was made whole from that hour" (Matthew 9:22).

One verse shows the relationship between faith and justification (Romans 5:1) and another between sin and death (v.12). As the student observes these detailed relationships he becomes increasingly aware of the unity of the Word of God.

Because the Holy Spirit guided the men who wrote the Scriptures many of its spiritual concepts are related. Sometimes these truths are located in different parts of the Bible. To discover and recognize these relationships should be a primary goal of Bible students. For example, Paul discusses the role of faith in the life of the believer (Romans 3; 4). James deals with the subject of works (James 2). Analyzing the passages separately is very enlightening, but a new appreciation of the total subject of faith and works is gained as the student compares the passages and observes the relationships.

Joy of Discovery

Observation that includes prayerful meditation results in the discovery of spiritual truth of which the Bible contains an inexhaustible supply. Diligent students of the Word have experienced the joy of discovering new truths or of rediscovering old ones.

Christians in past generations have felt the joy and

victory of discovering Biblical truths, but these truths are not automatically passed on to succeeding generations of believers. Some are communicated through Sunday school efforts, preaching and teaching ministry, and sharing, but many yield only to the study efforts of individual Christians. When you experience the joy of discovering truth you will also be excited about sharing it: "I will speak of thy testimonies also before kings, and will not be ashamed" (Psalm 119:46).

Interpretation

While observation tells what a verse says, interpretation gives its meaning. If observation has been thorough and systematic, interpretation will be accurate and meaningful. But Bible students who try to interpret a passage without thoroughly understanding what it says are not likely to get an accurate and complete meaning.

A prerequisite, then, for correct interpretation is accurate observation. Even in simple passages the student must carefully and prayerfully weigh all information before he accepts a meaning.

In striving to determine the meaning of a passage, the student must not use it merely to verify his prejudice or tradition. Remember that Biblical truth is independent of the human mind. We can discover and apply it but we can never create it. God's ways are higher than our ways (Isaiah 55:8, 9). Therefore, we should seek to understand His ways even when they conflict with ours.

The following principles are suggested as guidelines for interpretation:

First, observe carefully and systematically; only then can you find accurate meanings.

Flows From Analysis

Second, interpretation often flows from analysis. When a passage has been thoroughly examined and the student accurately understands what it says, the primary meaning often becomes immediately evident. However, because this occurs frequently the student should not assume it will happen every time. It can only occur when the complete meaning is inherent in the passage or context.

Often a passage has one primary interpretation but several applications. If, after careful analysis of a passage, the meaning remains unclear, don't be discouraged. The major teachings regarding salvation and the Christian life are simple and clear. But some profound areas yield meaning only after persistent and prayerful study.

Cross-referencing

Third, when the interpretation does not yield to thorough analysis of the passage and context, the student should examine related verses in other parts of the Bible. Often this will shed light on the subject and result in discovering the proper meaning. For instance, the complete meaning of Psalm 22 can be determined only when you analyze it in connection with Matthew 27.

Do not interpret a verse or passage in isolation. Study it in its context along with all other related passages. A broader scope of meaning results from this process.

More Than Analysis

Employing all the mechanics of scientific study is not enough for the student of the Scriptures. These methods are effective only when accompanied by earnest prayer and complete dependence on the Holy Spirit. We might well pray as did the Psalmist: "Make me to understand the way of thy precepts" (Psalm 119:27).

Application

Bible study should be considered as a continuous process. By it we learn and grow.

As the student gains new meaning and understanding of Biblical truth, he might ask himself: "How does this truth apply to me personally? How should I respond to it or what adjustments should be made in my life-style because of it?" Accompanying these questions should be a sincere and earnest prayer similar to one found in the Word of God: "Make me to go in the path of thy commandments; for therein do I delight" (Psalm 119:35).

The inductive approach to Bible study will be productive if you follow it carefully. Bible students using it consistently will accumulate a rich understanding of spiritual truth. This truth has two major purposes: First, it should be shared with others. Second, to be of personal value we need to make a personal application. This should be done prayerfully and immediately. Obedience should immediately follow enlightenment or revelation.

The Holy Spirit speaks to the individual Christian through personal study of the Word. If personal application seems difficult, ask God for divine help. God never asks us to accomplish anything without providing the necessary grace and strength! It is through the process of studying, learning, and making personal application of Biblical truth that we grow in spiritual stature.

11

Something About Everything

We live in an issue-oriented society. It seems everybody has a pet topic. Environmentalists are vocal in expressing concern about pure water and clean air. Health faddists strongly recommend certain kinds of natural foods. But topics come and go. The highly emotional issues of the immediate past are rarely discussed by the same groups or by the news media today.

The topical approach to study has long been popular among Bible students. D. L. Moody stated:

> One of the best ways to study the Scriptures is to study them topically. Merely reading the Bible is no use at all unless we study it thoroughly. Read as if you were seeking for something of value. It is a good deal better to take a single chapter and spend a month on it than to read the Bible at random for a month.

What's Topical Study?

Although most students are familiar with the topical approach, a few statements about it might be helpful. This method differs from other approaches to Bible study because the student begins with a subject rather than a passage of Scripture. He searches the Bible for verses or passages related to the chosen topic.

Like most systematic study methods, the topical

approach has a definite step-by-step plan to follow.

Choosing a Topic

The first step, of course, is to choose a topic. Choosing a topic for study should be done prayerfully. Why? Isn't any subject in the Bible important enough to study at any given time? In a general sense we must answer yes. But there are other principles that qualify this statement.

Because God knows your immediate and future needs, it is wise to ask Him for guidance as you select a topic for study. The Scriptures declare that He will give guidance to His people: "He leads the humble in the right way and teaches them his will. With faithfulness and love he leads all who keep his covenant and obey his commands" (Psalm 25:9, 10, *Good News Bible*, TEV). So, ask God to guide you in choosing a subject.

The purpose of Bible study will help determine the topic. If the major goal is personal development, interest and need are important factors. A word of caution: Selection of subjects for study should be broader in scope than those involving interest and conscious need. A balance of topics should be included over a period of time so you will gain Biblical knowledge in all important areas. But interest and need are critical factors in making a choice. Sometimes it is God's way of leading us into spiritual truth that will meet a present or future need.

If the study involves a group, their needs should be considered. The topical approach is used very effectively by groups.

The Word of God abundantly meets human needs. How can we know this? What assurance do we have that the Word meets human needs? The Bible declares it. The Word of God meets human needs for truth (John 17:17); joy (Jeremiah 15:16); lamp and light (Psalm 119:105); help in temptation (v. 11); faith (Romans 10:17); healing (Psalm 107:20); spiritual food (1 Peter 2:2); cleansing (John 15:3); hope (Psalm 119:81); and rejoicing (v. 162).

So choose a topic prayerfully, giving careful consideration to personal and group needs and interests. Also strive for balanced treatment of the subject.

Gathering the Scripture References

The second step after deciding on a topic is to gather the Scripture references. As the investigation proceeds the student will soon realize that some subjects are represented by numerous passages while others have only a few. Even some important doctrinal subjects are represented by a relatively few verses. You should not judge the importance of a topic by its numerical representation.

If a topic is represented by a few passages, it is crucial to include all of them. In cases where the number is too large to include them all, key passages should be selected to represent every area of the subject. Caution: Often verses and concepts left out of a study are as significant as those included. All areas of a subject need to be examined and studied if you are to gain a thorough understanding.

Most cults and false doctrines are based on a few isolated passages that are interpreted to substantiate personal prejudice and opinion. One sure way to avoid this type of error is to include in the study all the Scripture references on a given subject.

Fortunately, there are many excellent reference materials available to students using this approach. Many Bibles contain a rather comprehensive concordance, usually located in a section toward the back. Any good concordance will list most Scripture references on a given topic. Another valuable tool is a topical textbook in which subjects are listed in alphabetical order along with the major Scripture passages.

To illustrate, let us select some passages on the subject of prayer:

Prayer

1. Immediate answer at times (Isaiah 65:24)
2. Answer beyond expectation (Ephesians 3:20)
3. Falling on face in prayer (Numbers 16:22)
4. Making supplication (Job 8:5)
5. Seeking the face of the Lord (Psalm 27:8)
6. Pouring out the soul (1 Samuel 1:15)
7. Answer different from our expectation at times (2 Corinthians 12:8, 9)
8. Kneeling in prayer (Acts 20:36)
9. Drawing near to God (Hebrews 10:22)
10. Calling on the Lord (Genesis 12:8)
11. Answer delayed at times (Luke 18:7)
12. Bowing down (Psalm 95:6)
13. Pouring out the heart (Psalm 62:8)
14. Answer granted through faith (James 1:5, 6)
15. Standing (Mark 11:25)

These 15 references cover several areas. Undoubtedly you would include many more to give a comprehensive view. In a subject as broad as prayer the student should use Scripture passages from both the Old and New Testaments.

Organizing Is Important

The new pastor had served the church less than a

year. During that time he had carefully prepared his sermons and Bible-teaching outlines. He was meticulous. His assumption was that people would benefit from his ministry if they clearly understood what he said. A further assumption was that if his people were to understand his sermons, the content would need to be carefully organized.

Although he consciously made efforts to simplify his messages, he was never sure about achieving his goal until a teenage girl approached him following a Sunday morning service. During the conversation she commented: "Pastor, I really enjoy your sermons. They are all so easy to understand. In fact, I take notes on them and use the outlines in speaking to the youth groups."

Organizing your material, which is the fourth step, can make the difference between a clear understanding and a vague, confused picture of the subject. When a topic is not viewed or presented in a logical and organized manner, the human mind has difficulty with perception and memory. But good organization facilitates both perception and memory.

Consider again the 15 references on prayer. For illustrative purposes let us divide them into a more logical order using subtopics.

Prayer

1. Prayer Described as
   a. Calling on the Lord (Genesis 12:8)
   b. Drawing near to God (Hebrews 10:22)
   c. Pouring out the heart (Psalm 62:8)
   d. Pouring out the soul (1 Samuel 1:15)
   e. Seeking the face of the Lord (Psalm 27:8)
   f. Making supplication (Job 8:5)
2. Posture in Prayer

  a. Standing (Mark 11:25)
  b. Bowing down (Psalm 95:6)
  c. Kneeling in prayer (Acts 20:36)
  d. Falling on face in prayer (Numbers 16:22)
 3. Answers to Prayer Granted
  a. Immediate answer at times (Isaiah 65:24)
  b. Answer delayed at times (Luke 18:7)
  c. Answer different from our expectation at times (2 Corinthians 12:8, 9)
  d. Answer beyond expectation (Ephesians 3:20)
  e. Answer granted through faith (James 1:5, 6)

As indicated by the outline, we divided the topic into three subtopics. If our study was comprehensive there would be other subtopics such as: why prayer isn't answered, when to pray, great prayers of the Bible, and many others. Some subjects with limited references may have fewer or no subtopics.

Analyzing Is a Must

 The fifth step in the topical approach to Bible study is to analyze the material you have gathered and outlined. The prime factor in the analysis process is complete reliance on the Spirit's illuminating power. Human reason alone is inadequate.

 Analyzing simply means to look carefully and prayerfully at the Scripture passages you have gathered. Then organize them with the purpose of finding factual material that will lead to meanings, seeing relationships, discovering spiritual concepts, and making personal applications.

 For example, look again at subtopic #2, posture in prayer. Let us assume we have listed all the references. While we read the individual passages we notice that people prayed in several different physical postures. We begin to see that posture is not always an important factor in prayer. This may come as a surprise to Christians who are accustomed to praying while in a predetermined physical position, such as kneeling. It might lead the student to ask: "If posture isn't an important factor in prayer, what is?" A spin-off topic like this could lead to the very heart of the major subject of prayer.

Drawing Conclusions

What shall we do with the information we get from collecting, organizing, and analyzing Scripture references? This question is answered by the sixth step, drawing conclusions. In some ways analyzing the material and drawing conclusions are similar, and sometimes they may be the same function. Usually, however, analysis identifies information while the conclusion phase organizes and interprets it.

Conclusions are the significant principles drawn from the mass of factual material accumulated by the study. Each individual Scripture passage listed under a subtopic is a truth in itself. Usually it is one aspect of a broader spiritual concept that can be identified only by collecting and analyzing all passages on the selected topic.

It is in this area where the adherents of cults and false doctrines err. They build a major doctrine on one or possibly a few passages. Their error is made by expanding the truth found in a single Scripture passage beyond what God intended. Fundamental doctrines can be stated accurately and Biblically only after all related passages are carefully studied. G. Raymond Carlson in commenting on this states:

> There is error in teaching a doctrine with only a few selected texts. . . . When we gain proper emphasis and understanding of all the Bible teaches on a given topic,

we will be kept from error and grounded in the truth *(How to Study the Bible* [Springfield, Mo: Gospel Publishing House, 1964], p. 63).

But what are Christians to do with the conclusions resulting from their study? First, they should be organized in written form so they can be easily shared with groups or individuals. Second, a personal application should be made of the truth. This introduces the last step in the topical approach.

Application

To search out and identify Biblical truth is a spiritual blessing, but if it is to be fully effective one must make a personal application. Positive changes in attitudes, temperament, behavior, and relationships should be the result. This process often involves a willingness to make deeper and broader commitments to God.

The Scriptures reveal God's will to us. Sometimes His plan is to bring about changes in our lives. Some of these changes may involve long-established habits. But the Word of God is able to discern clearly and accurately what our needs for improvement are (Hebrews 4:12).

It is essential to understand how the truth relates personally to the individual Christian, but it takes commitment to apply it and to make the necessary personal adjustments that should follow. This requires prayer and close fellowship with God. It cannot be accomplished by human endeavor alone. Jesus said: "Watch and pray, that ye enter not into temptation: the spirit indeed is willing, but the flesh is weak" (Matthew 26:41).

Often the success of Bible study pivots on personal application. Prayer creates an attitude of willingness in the believer's heart. Only then can truth be applied effectively to bring the life into conformity to God's will.

Advantages and Disadvantages

The topical approach has some definite advantages and a few disadvantages. Some truths, such as doctrine, lend themselves well to the topical approach. Name the doctrine and any good concordance will list all Scripture references. Then the student can follow each step in the topical study method. This helps the student get a comprehensive view.

The ease with which we can treat subjects that reflect current needs is another strength of this method. When a special need arises that demands an answer, gathering all related passages is made relatively simple by the multitude of helps available, such as concordances and topical textbooks. It matters not whether the need pertains to an individual, a local church, or a prayer group.

The topical approach has some weaknesses. They do not render it ineffective, but they should be kept in mind by students who use this method.

One major weakness is that the topical approach does not cover the Bible systematically. This has special significance for those who use it frequently. The student who is not careful could become unbalanced in his beliefs and emphases.

Caution also needs to be taken so that pet subjects are not studied exclusively. Students should strive for balance in doctrine and emphasis.

The topical method of Bible study can be most productive when it is used wisely; taking advantage of its strengths and avoiding its weaknesses.

12

But Who Is Zerubbabel?

It is a difficult word to pronounce. But who was he and why is his name listed in the Bible? If he was an important person, what did he do that made his life outstanding? I wonder how many times he is mentioned in the Scriptures? Is he remembered because of performing good deeds or wicked ones? But how can I ever learn to pronounce his name? Z-E-R-U-B-B-A-B-E-L! All these questions and more were running through the mind of a young husband as he and his wife sat in the young marrieds' class. They hadn't been Christians too long and were eager to learn.

The Sunday school lessons that quarter focused on the message found in the Old Testament Book of Ezra. They centered on the proclamation of Cyrus and his provision for rebuilding the temple in Jerusalem. The teacher had prepared the lesson thoroughly and included a biographical study of Zerubbabel. A profitable discussion took place that not only answered the young man's questions but provided many other interesting insights.

The biography is another approach to Bible study. It has been used for centuries by students wanting to learn more about how God used men to promote His work on earth. But what is a biography? In simple terms a biography is a written account of a person's life. The Word of God is filled with biographical accounts of men and women.

People are fascinating. Observing them in a crowded shopping center or reading about their lives is always an interesting experience. Magazines, newspapers, and periodicals of all types include feature stories about the lives of people.

God has chosen to give much of His Word in biographical form. If all the stories involving the lives of men and women were removed from the Bible, there would be little left to read. God in His wisdom used a method that would capture our interest.

A biography is interesting to read. But what value is it to Christians? What spiritual help and blessing can we expect to receive from it? Although interest is an important factor, literature must have other qualities if the reader is to gain spiritual benefits. Let us consider some of the benefits one can gain by reading the biographies recorded in the Bible.

Why Read Biographies?

"Now these things befell them by way of a figure—as an example and warning [to us]; they were written to admonish and fit us for right action by good instruction, we in whose days the ages have reached their climax—their consummation and concluding period" (1 Corinthians 10:11, *Amplified*). So the Bible gives us the major reason for using biographies. The Holy Spirit, by the pen of Paul, tells us they are written for our examples.

Educators are placing increasing emphasis on the significance a model plays in the learning process. The influence of a model can be either negative or positive. The biographical accounts of men and women in the Bible demonstrate both good and evil.

111

But most encouraging are the stories of men and women who won great victories through faith and obedience. It is delightful to witness God's blessings being poured out upon the lives of individuals who obey Him (Deuteronomy 11:26, 27).

The lives of some ended in tragedy. Cain, Nadab, Absalom, and Demas are only a few whose lives climaxed in great sorrow. Why? Because they did not obey God (v. 28). The Christian today who studies these accounts can profit much as he clearly sees the abundant blessing that results from obedience and the judgment that follows disobedience.

They Inspire Us Too

It was an exceptionally large gathering. The chamber of commerce in a large city had invited a professional football player as guest speaker. He was well known since millions saw him often during football season. His athletic skills were admired by many as they watched him perform on TV.

As he ended his address the applause was loud and long. Standing for one last word before the banquet ended, he apologized for his need to leave immediately because of another commitment. He couldn't even sign autographs. What the admiring crowd didn't learn until later was the nature of his commitment. Knowing he would be in this particular city, he volunteered to give his personal testimony at one of the rescue missions. What a hero! How inspirational it is to learn about men whose lives are dedicated to the cause of Christ.

The Bible has its lists of heroes too:

> And what shall I more say? for the time would fail me to tell of Gideon, and of Barak, and of Samson, and of Jephthah; of David also, and Samuel, and of the

prophets: who through faith subdued kingdoms, wrought righteousness, obtained promises, stopped the mouths of lions, quenched the violence of fire, escaped the edge of the sword, out of weakness were made strong, waxed valiant in fight, turned to flight the armies of the aliens (Hebrews 11:32-34).

Isn't it marvelous that people of all ages can find inspiration and courage by reading the biographies of these servants of God? Children love the story of David. They never tire of hearing about how he tended sheep, fought Goliath, and tried to wear Saul's armor.

Timothy and John Mark in the New Testament also capture the attention of teenagers. Going against the tide of sin and wickedness in their day was no easy task. They often faced hardship and possible death. Young people are quick to recognize the qualities of courage and spiritual strength they manifested.

Older Christians too are inspired to deeper faith and courage to face trials by reading the Biblical accounts of men and women of faith. Although none of these faithful servants of God was perfect, great inspiration is derived from reading about them.

They Demonstrate God's Mercy

"For as the heaven is high above the earth, so great is his mercy toward them that fear him" (Psalm 103:11). God never condones sin in any form. But according to the Scriptures everyone has sinned (Romans 3:23). This all-inclusive statement is a universal indictment. But wait—although God cannot tolerate sin He infinitely loves the sinner. He provided a way for sinful men to be cleansed and accepted into His great family.

After King David had strayed from God and committed a series of deplorable acts, thereby breaking fellowship with God, he prayed: "Have mercy upon me, O God, according to thy loving-kindness: according unto the multitude of thy tender mercies blot out my transgressions" (Psalm 51:1). A study of the lives of all great men and women in the Bible reveals God's tender mercies to man.

Judgment Is Real Too

Biblical biographies also demonstrate God's judgment. While God delights in showing mercy and love, His judgment must inevitably follow unrepented sin and disobedience: "But, after thy hardness and impenitent heart, treasurest up unto thyself wrath against the day of wrath and revelation of the righteous judgment of God" (Romans 2:5).

When we study these biographies it is important to remember we are viewing portraits of human beings. They were just as human as we are. Consequently, we must take into account God's true estimate of them. This should not lower them in our thinking; rather, it should magnify the grace of God.

The biographies of the Bible have a spiritual value above all other biographies for they relate to us the reactions of human nature to divine matters. From these lessons we learn how to avoid similar pitfalls and to better adjust our lives to God's will.

What's the Procedure?

A Bible college instructor had completed his introduction to the biographical approach to Bible study. Because it was an area of special interest, his enthusiasm proved contagious. The class was highly motivated and eager to begin their studies. One stu-

114

dent seemed puzzled. After commenting on the value and interest factor of biographical studies, he posed an interesting and significant question: "To gain the most from studying the lives of great men and women in the Bible what would be a good procedure to follow?"

We may follow several guidelines when we employ the biographical approach to Bible study.

Assemble All References

First, assemble all references on the character to be studied. Sometimes these references are found scattered throughout the Bible. In cases where most of them are concentrated in one chapter or Book, it is still important to consult the isolated ones. Often they contribute significantly to our insight into the person's character and life.

Be cautious during this process because several different Biblical characters sometimes have the same name. The student must exercise care and discrimination as he gathers references.

To illustrate these principles let us briefly study the life of Jacob. What an interesting life he lived. It was a blend of victory and defeat, sorrow and gladness, success and failure, but through it all he served God. Jacob is mentioned 390 times in the Bible, 366 times in the Old Testament and 24 times in the New.

Names Have Meanings

Second, determine the meaning of the person's name. A Biblical name often was an expression of a significant characteristic of the person. New and meaningful insights are gained by carefully examining the person's name.

What is the special significance of the name Jacob? Jacob means cheater, supplanter, or deceiver (Genesis 25:26). In doing a biographical study of Jacob the student will readily discern why the name was appropriate. Later as Jacob's relationship with God developed and matured, there was a corresponding change in his life-style. He became increasingly aware of his dependence on God. Being human he continued to make mistakes, but God decided to give him another name—Israel. This new name reflected God's estimation of him for it means "a prince . . . with God" (32:28).

Examine Background Information

Third, examine the background of the person. Trace his ancestry if possible. Where was he born? What kind of educational background did he have? Were the home and community influences positive or negative?

Jacob was the son of Isaac and the grandson of Abraham. Jacob and Esau were twins. Although they were good people, Isaac and Rebekah as parents seemed to make more than their share of mistakes. Parental favoritism was a major factor contributing to the ill feelings that existed between Jacob and Esau for much of their lives (Genesis 27:1-29).

Observe the deceptive actions. Isaac craftily arranged for Esau to prepare a banquet (vv. 1-4); Rebekah plotted to foil Isaac (vv. 5-10); and Jacob's lack of faith in God to fulfill His word (25:23) caused him to become a deceiver (27:11-13).

What Kind of Associates?

Sometimes we can gain valuable insights by learning about the person's intimate friends and associates. There is some validity to the cliche: "Birds of a feather flock together." People who voluntarily associate with each other usually have some common interests, problems, or goals. Discovering these often leads to valuable information about them.

So, as the fourth step, make a survey of the Biblical character's friends and associates.

Jacob had many friends throughout his life. Because of his trickery and deceit he had to flee from his home and friends. He found refuge with his Uncle Laban. There he was deceived and served 14 years for Rachel's hand instead of the 7 he had planned. His wages were changed 10 times in 20 years.

Character Traits

Fifth, carefully observe the individual's particular character traits. How did he respond to different situations? to different people? Was he decisive or did he vacillate? Was his behavior impulsive or based on reason?

Jacob by nature was a cheater and supplanter. Many of his personal troubles stemmed from the expression of this trait. But Jacob was much more than this. He had a deep appreciation for spiritual values. The birthright and blessing were of great value to him. Most important, he had a heart that was tender toward God.

Failures and Shortcomings

Although we don't recommend dwelling on failures, a survey of them can be very instructive and informative. Why did a particular individual fail and what steps led to it? How did these failures affect him and those around him?

117

What about Jacob? Wasn't he a failure? Yes, he had many shortcomings and failed to take the right action in many cases. He tricked Esau out of his birthright (Genesis 25:27-34). He actually stole the blessing by deceiving Isaac (27:1-33). He outwitted Laban with superb animal husbandry (30:25-43). Jacob continued to deceive others until he was transformed at Peniel. But he continued to suffer throughout his life because of his wrongdoings.

A Crisis Experience

Most people during their lifetime experience several outstanding crises. How they react to them often results in major changes in their life-style. The seventh step is to identify these critical experiences.

While Jacob had many crises, a major one occurred at Peniel. Twenty years had passed between his experience with God at Bethel and his experience at Peniel where he wrestled with God. But when Jacob submitted, his name was changed to Israel, a prince with God.

What Did He Contribute?

The eighth step is to determine what contributions the individual made to his time and ours.

Jacob became a primary link in the human family that led to the birth of Jesus Christ, our Saviour. The example he set in crying out to God in times of crisis has been valuable to people of every generation.

Main Lesson

Finally, we should seek to identify the main lesson of the character's life and understand its particular value to us. How can we benefit from it?

In Jacob's case it is difficult to decide what the main lesson is. There are many. But two seem to stand out. First, his life clearly demonstrates what God can do with a human life even though it is plagued with failure, if the person's heart is tender toward Him. And, second, Jacob's life is a warning to those whose lives are not characterized by obedience to God. Untold suffering and heartache are experienced unnecessarily by Christians who are not careful to walk according to God's will.

13

Making It All Meaningful

For a number of years a mature Christian couple living in the Midwest had dreamed of visiting California but couldn't because of family responsibilities. Now with their children grown and married, their dream was about to come true. They had saved enough money to take the trip and were excitedly planning it.

During several hours of consultation with the local travel bureau, they discovered that not only was there a variety of modes of transportation available, but also several interesting scenic routes.

But what does a Bible student have in common with this couple? Just as they became aware of travel options, so the student learns there are many effective approaches to Bible study—and all lead through scenic country.

Bible study should be one of the Christian's most productive and rewarding experiences. But why does it appear to be more meaningful to some Christians than others?

Study Plus Prayer Plus Praise

For maximum effectiveness, Bible study should be one component of a balanced Christian approach to worship. It will take on new and enriched meaning when it is accompanied by prayer and praise: "While I live will I praise the LORD: I will sing praises unto my God while I have any being" (Psalm 146:2).

Prayer is a two-way communication system. It places the individual in a very intimate relationship with God. We gaze with awe and wonder at this most hallowed relationship: a finite human being communicating with the infinite God! Praise, adoration, worship, and thankfulness emanate from deep within the individual's being. Fellowship with God through consistent prayer, praise, and worship keeps the heart tender and receptive. It also creates a frame of mind conducive to accepting and receiving spiritual truth.

When accompanied by Bible study, prayer and praise effect a refining work in the believer's life and the fruit of the Spirit begin to develop and overflow to the praise and glory of God.

Permeate Your Being

The mind, heart, soul, spirit, and life-style should be deeply affected and influenced by the Word. Many Christians are sadly unaware of the scope of its work. The writer of the Book of Hebrews gives a vivid description of the Word as it operates within a person's life:

> For the Word that God speaks is alive and full of power—making it active, operative, energizing and effective; it is sharper than any two-edged sword, penetrating to the dividing line of the breath of life (soul) and [the immortal] spirit, and of joints and marrow [that is, of the deepest parts of our nature] exposing and sifting and analyzing and judging the very thoughts and purposes of the heart (4:12, *Amplified*).

So open your life completely to the Bible. Let its

teachings and wisdom move beyond the mental sphere so your whole being is affected by its power.

Give It High Priority

Why do we choose to engage in certain activities while refusing or neglecting to participate in others? Our selection of activities is based on the priority rating we assign it. Although we may not always be conscious of why we decide on a specific activity, our actions tell the story.

In the lives of earnest Christians Bible study is a high priority. They integrate it into their pattern of everyday living. Even when their days are filled with stress and increased activity, they read and honor the Bible. One writer of Scripture declared: "I will delight myself in thy statutes: I will not forget thy word" (Psalm 119:16).

It is a historical fact that in communities and nations where the Word of God is given high priority, the quality of life is increased. The Word has an uplifting effect on individuals, groups, or countries that honor it. Make your encounter with the Word of God consistent.

Believe It All

"Jesus saith unto him, Go thy way; thy son liveth. And the man believed the word that Jesus had spoken unto him, and he went his way" (John 4:50). Here is a man who experienced a miracle simply because he heard and believed the words of Jesus. His son was near the point of death but was raised up because his father believed! The great truths of Scripture become personally effective only when we believe them.

It is unfortunate that some very fine Christians do

not believe that miracles beyond salvation occur to-day. To them manifestations of God's power to perform the miraculous are restricted to apostolic times. But the Scriptures declare that Jesus Christ is "the same yesterday, and today, and for ever" (Hebrews 13:8). Although the Christian may not always seek miracles, when the need arises his faith doesn't restrict God's method of operation.

You will be amazed and thrilled at what God will do when you believe all the Scriptures. Some glorious experiences the Bible declares are for the believer are: salvation; the healing of body, mind, and emotions; the baptism in the Holy Spirit with the evidence of speaking in tongues; the operation of the gifts of the Spirit; and power over evil forces. Why believe God for anything less? It pleases God when the Holy Spirit can operate, unhindered by unbelief, through His followers. Believe all the Scriptures. Don't restrict God by a limited interpretation of the Bible.

Scope of Its Influence

One amazing and exciting phase of Bible study is viewing the broad scope of the Bible's influence on the lives of people. It is more than just another book; it is the revelation of God to man. When we believe and apply it, it affects every area of our lives. Our attitudes are changed and new thinking patterns are developed. Our life-style is revolutionized and Jesus Christ becomes preeminent.

The findings of a national youth survey conducted by George Edgerly are not only interesting but enlightening. Some of the responses discussed in the following paragraphs are illustrative of the positive effects consistent Bible study has on young people.

First, young people who regularly engaged in personal Bible study and private devotions were higher in spiritual status than others of the group.

Second, engaged and married youth called for stronger emphasis on the study of Biblical views of sexuality, morals, dating, courtship, and preparation for marriage and establishing a Christian home.

Third, the young person's participation in family devotions had an impact on his spiritual status and also contributed to positive family relationships.

Fourth, generally the quality of life was significantly higher for those who consistently studied the Bible. Their philosophy of life was healthier and more positive.

Share Its Blessings

After Jesus delivered a man from demon powers He sent him away saying: "Return to thine own house, and show how great things God hath done unto thee. And he went his way, and published throughout the whole city how great things Jesus had done unto him" (Luke 8:39).

The more a Christian shares the blessings of God's Word, the richer and more meaningful they become to him. Every Christian has the opportunity to share them at some level. It is helpful to carry a small New Testament with you. Then prayerfully ask God to provide opportunities to share. Begin with family members and close friends. People generally are interested in good news. What better news could there possibly be than the personal blessings that result from contact with the Word of God?

The New Testament contains several moving illustrations of sharing. Andrew had just met Jesus.

John the Baptist had called attention to Him. After visiting with Jesus, Andrew couldn't wait to find his brother Simon Peter and share this good news with him. Philip was elated by his contact with Jesus. Almost bursting with excitement and joy, he sought out Nathanael to share with him the experience of meeting Jesus of Nazareth (John 1:35-45).

Claim Its Promises

"Whereby are given unto us exceeding great and precious promises; that by these ye might be partakers of the divine nature, having escaped the corruption that is in the world through lust" (2 Peter 1:4).

One fact that becomes increasingly evident to Bible students is the variety and number of promises God made to His people. They're so obvious, but often go unnoticed by many Christians. An encouraging and exciting aspect of God's promises is that they cover every area of human need. The ill, the lonely, the discouraged, those saddened by adverse circumstances, or even the defeated will find promises in the Bible that offer God's remedy for their situation. No wonder Peter referred to them as "exceeding great and precious promises."

But why do so many Christians live far below their privileges as sons and daughters of God? Why do we sometimes accept adverse conditions or situations in life as inevitable when God has promised deliverance? or suffer deprivation when God has promised to supply? We are not referring to the trials and testings God permits us to experience. Although unpleasant, these are for our good; they are designed to increase the quality of our spiritual lives.

It pleases God when his people manifest implicit trust in His Word. By claiming His promises for deliverance, provision, healing, or any need, we are expressing confidence in Him. What God says is true. His promises are not empty words.

Bible study becomes alive and meaningful when a Christian makes this kind of application. The promises are real. We must claim them and accept God's provision for us. Until we do, God's Word is not as effective as He intended it to be in accomplishing His purposes in our lives.

Obey Its Teachings

A vast knowledge of the Word of God without a heart that is inclined to obey accomplishes little in a believer's life. The Bible will become meaningful and effective only as we obey it. "Be ye doers of the word, and not hearers only, deceiving your own selves" (James 1:22).

An account in 1 Samuel vividly illustrates the premium God places on obedience. The Lord through Samuel told King Saul to completely destroy the Amalekites. The instructions were precise and clear. Even the cattle, sheep, and camels were to be slain. Not a remnant was to be spared.

In the battle Saul and his soldiers prevailed. Only the enemy King Agag remained, along with some of the best animals. Saul disregarded the instructions of Samuel and spared Agag and some of the best animals, claiming he intended to use them for a sacrifice unto the Lord. But take note of God's answer: "And Samuel said, Hath the LORD as great delight in burnt offerings and sacrifices, as in obeying the voice of the LORD? Behold, to obey is better than sacrifice, and to hearken than the fat of rams" (15:22).

Acknowledge Its Author

"For the prophecy came not in old time by the will

of man: but holy men of God spake as they were moved by the Holy Ghost" (2 Peter 1:21). Although God used human instruments to speak and write, He was ultimately the Author. For instance, the apostle John ministered for a number of years and may have written many letters but only specific ones became part of the Bible. Even Paul spoke many words and wrote many letters during his lifetime, but only selected teachings became Scripture.

Why? Because God in His wisdom knew what instructions and teachings present and future generations needed. Therefore, the Holy Spirit moved upon men to record only the words, sentences, and teachings that God designed to become Scripture.

Follow the Rules

To make Bible study meaningful the student must carefully follow established rules of interpretation. Because interpretation has been discussed in another chapter, we will take note only of several pertinent Scripture passages at this point.

First, "rightly dividing the word of truth" is a must (2 Timothy 2:15). But what does "rightly dividing" mean? To rightly divide means to search out the correct meaning and make a true application to the different times and classes of people. All Bible study pivots on this—discovering the meaning the Holy Spirit intended to convey and making the proper application.

Second, the Word declares that no prophecy of Scripture is of personal or private interpretation (2 Peter 1:20). This is another way of saying that only the true meaning of a Scripture passage should be accepted. The meaning cannot be changed or altered to fit a given situation. Students should guard against going beyond the truth the Holy Spirit intended to convey, even though it might seem harmless.

The Word Enriches

Bible study again is much more than a mental process. The intellect is important, but mere accumulation of Biblical facts is not God's design: "Let the word of Christ dwell in you richly in all wisdom" (Colossians 3:16). God's design is for the Word to dwell in us and enrich our lives—not just the intellect, but our total being. Spirit, soul, body, and mind are made rich by the indwelling Word.

Don't Forget Its Power

A power-conscious world is threatened by the growing energy shortage. Without the power provided by energy the wheels of industry would stop. Economies would crumble. Transportation would come to a standstill and man would face a crisis that defied solution.

For Christians the Bible is an inexhaustible source of spiritual power. It provides power to be born again (1 Peter 1:23); power to keep us from sinning (Psalm 119:11); power to cause rejoicing (v. 162); and power to uphold all things (Hebrews 1:3).

So, don't be shortchanged in Bible study. Make it meaningful. Choose an approach, select a Book or passage, and get off to a good start. Read it, believe it, apply it, and live it. Let the Word dwell in you richly, affecting all areas of your life. Then, share it with others.